# The Southern Way

The regular volume for the Southern devotee

Kevin Robertson

## Issue 48

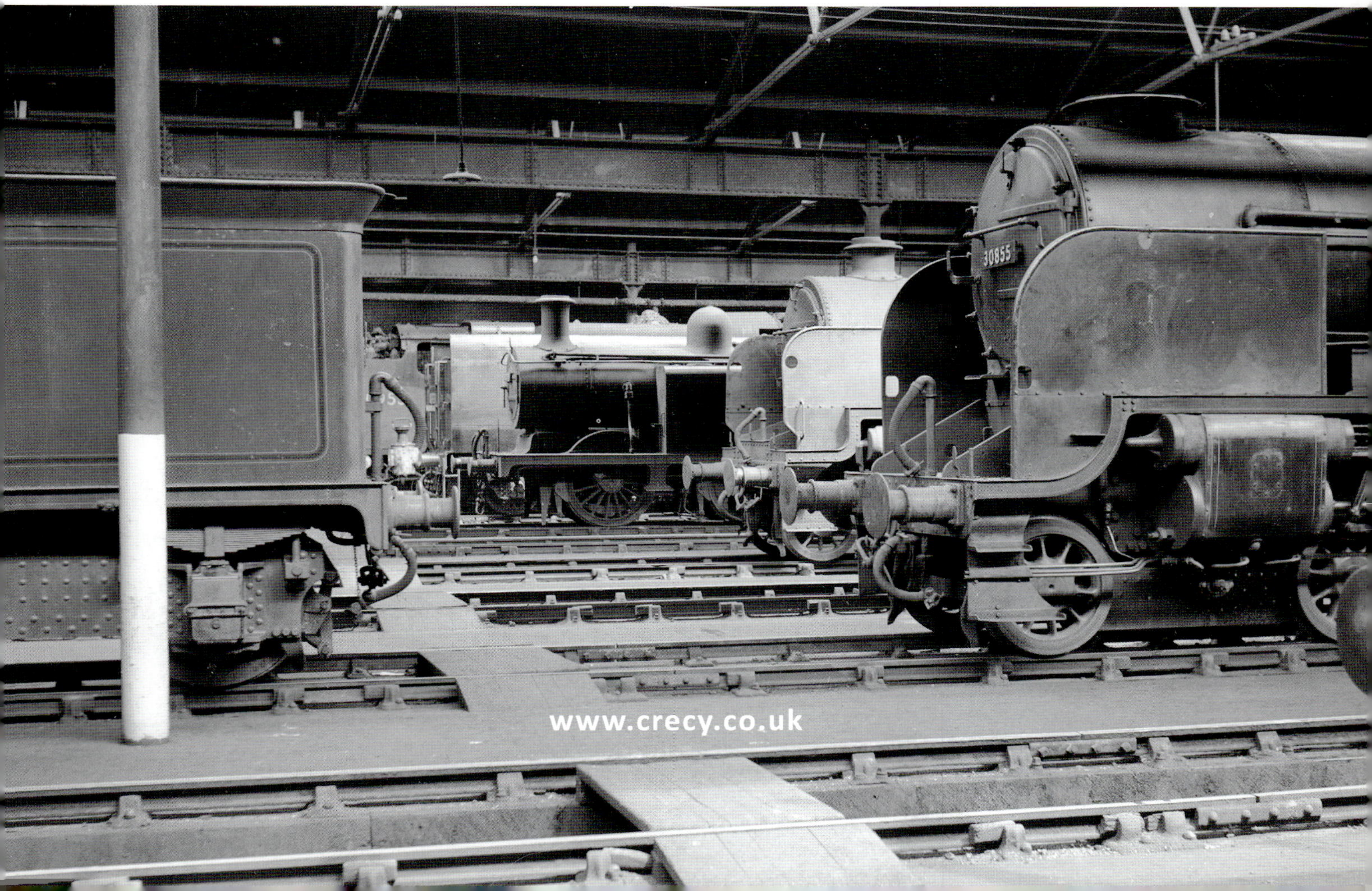

www.crecy.co.uk

© 2019 Crécy Publishing Ltd
and the various contributors

ISBN 9781909328891

First published in 2019 by Noodle Books
an imprint of Crécy Publishing Ltd

**New contact details**
**All editorial submissions to:**
The Southern Way (Kevin Robertson)
**'Silmaril'**
**Upper Lambourn**
**Hungerford**
**Berkshire RG17 8QR**
Tel: 01488 674143
editorial@thesouthernway.co.uk

All rights reserved. No part of this book may be reproduced or transmitted in any form or by any means electronic or mechanical, including photocopying, recording or by any information storage without permission from the Publisher in writing. All enquiries should be directed to the Publisher.

A CIP record for this book is available from the British Library

Publisher's note: Every effort has been made to identify and correctly attribute photographic credits. Any error that may have occurred is entirely unintentional.

Printed in the UK by Short Run Press Ltd

**Noodle Books is an imprint of**
**Crécy Publishing Limited**
1a Ringway Trading Estate
Shadowmoss Road
Manchester M22 5LH

**www.crecy.co.uk**

**Issue No 49 of THE SOUTHERN WAY**
**ISBN 9781909328945**
**available in January 2020 at £14.95**

To receive your copy the moment it is released, order in advance from your usual supplier, or it can be sent post-free (UK) direct from the publisher:

Crécy Publishing Ltd (Noodle Books)

1a Ringway Trading Estate, Shadowmoss Road, Manchester M22 5LH

Tel 0161 499 0024

**www.crecy.co.uk**

enquiries@crecy.co.uk

*Front cover:*
**Before the days of pipelines, and compliant with the regulations for barrier wagons, Class 33 D6526 takes empty tank cars through Southampton Central *en route* to Fawley. The low sun also accentuates the numerous tiny creases and marks on what was little more than thin sheet around the front of the cab.** *Richard Simmons*

*Rear cover:*
**Hardly the correct train for an 'Alton – Eastleigh' pull-push headcode, so we are left to ponder on Standard Class 4 No 80147 in the down main platform at Eastleigh attached to a Bulleid '3-set'.**

*Title page:*
**Not totally confirmed but almost certainly this is the interior of Eastleigh and shows the correct practice of keeping the walkways clear. Memory has it there were at least three of these throughout the length of the shed supplemented by signs warning of the perils of attempting to jump across the pits. Even so people did (your Editor did) – but he was a lot younger and more agile and managed to get away with it at the time. In this scene, we suspect we are in the early 1950s in which nothing stirs and all appears quiet and calm – a Sunday perhaps? Looking back I never gave a thought to what maintenance the track may have received or was it still the original from half a century before – an interesting view as well of the wooden keys protruding from either side.**

# Contents

Introduction .................................................. 4

The Kent Coal Industry ............................... 6
   John Perkin

Nostalgia at Portsmouth ........................... 15
   Sean Bolan

Victorian Boom and Bust ........................... 18
   Railway Mania and the Bank of
   Overend Gurney
   John Burgess

A 'Britannia' at Portsmouth and North Camp ...... 31
   Images by Paul Cooper

Pat Harmer, Polegate Signalman ..................... 34
   Interviewed by David Vaughan

(More) Southern Railway Inspections ................ 44
   Compiled by Gerry Nichols

Southampton Central to Redbridge .................. 49
   Peter Tatlow

'Rebuilt' ...................................................... 55
   The Letters and Comments Pages

The Lost Archives of Stephen Townroe ............ 61
   Part 13

Interlude at Penshurst, 1966 ........................ 70
   Les Price

Len Mumford .............................................. 74
   A Railway Life
   Michael Rowe

Mr Drummond's LSWR 4-4-0s ........................ 85
   Jeremy Clarke

Back to the Future ..................................... 99

Book review ............................................. 103
   *LBSCR Carriages, Vol 3*
   *Bogie Stock 1879 – 1907*

# Introduction

Writing this in the early autumn of 2019, I recall back in May turning on the television and seeing a report on the end of HST working out of Paddington. 'The end of an era,' commented the reporter although he was also less than kind in referring to the trains as, 'old-fashioned, noisy and polluting.' I suppose on some counts he was right: yes, they are dated, certainly polluting, in that the power is produced on board instead of some power station elsewhere, and noisy – well far less than when originally introduced, new engines having helped with that. Funny how forty years ago they heralded in the 'new-age' and yet are now being castigated as belonging to history.

And I for one will miss them. They were a part of the everyday scene for decades and I have travelled many thousands of miles in them.

It is the same with steam and other such delights as the 4-CORs. Not quite so perhaps with the REPs/TCs, for that is purely a personal view, but I also miss the 442s and if the latter ever do enjoy a renaissance, I suspect the interiors will not be how I remember them. Strange then how we often fail to appreciate what is actually before us but then lament its very passing.

But we should not forget the HST will continue to perform, albeit in revised formation and the 442 may yet be resurrected, perhaps externally unaltered, but very different within. Which brings me to the point of this missive, just how much must remain for it to be classified as original – or is what we see in front of us today simply a set of new parts?

I know others have discussed this same topic before but I would like to reopen the discussion and invite others to have their say in future sections of 'Rebuilt'. Take the case of that grand set of people who are striving to 'unrebuild' No. 35011. Presumably the boiler, frames and wheels will be original (the interior of the boiler and the tyres perhaps not totally original), but when they succeed does this mean they now have an original 'MN'? Aesthetically perhaps, and I for one will be amongst the first to view the renaissance, but purely for the purpose of debate, at what point does it remain original or indeed start being new?

I recall the same discussion in some of the magazines of years ago, when a locomotive, steam/diesel/electric/unit – it matters not – is seen in the course of building with a number chalked on the side. Does a set of wheels alone constitute a 'cop' or does it need frames, a boiler/engine/traction motors/bodywork, etc. – the criteria is surely a matter of the opinion of the individual.

In the same way, is the recent fine recreation of a 'Saint' at Didcot, 'new-build' or renaissance using parts from other engines combined?

And I have to admit it is a long time since I wielded a spanner at a heritage railway (we called them preservation societies then), but even then I was struck by how many combinations of 'standard' parts stamped and then re-stamped went into an engine bearing a particular identification. This, it seems, applied to almost every railway company.

So when we see No 34xxx steaming along in the sunshine, is it really that actual engine or a mixture of old (meaning many different engines) and new? Indeed, is it really No. 34xxx at all? and in that I don't include the fashion for changing identities; if *Lord Nelson* masquerading as *Lord Howe* brings more 'bums on seats' to a railway, does it really matter anyway?

Finally, to reawaken the debate on original identities. We know the GWR did it and we know the LMS were also involved – in the GWR's case just once but the LMS did it twice; we mean the swapping of a locomotive's identity which subsequently became permanent. But does anyone know if the Southern (including BRS) ever did?

To conclude and on a totally different thread, I must relate some sad news; Alan Blackburn passed away in the spring. Alan was a mine of information especially on wagons and operation. He was co-author of the four books on LSWR, LBSCR, SECR and SR wagons and a more knowledgeable man it would be hard to find. We were also privileged to have him contribute both factually and in reminiscence form to 'SW'. Never one to accept inaccuracies, he was quick to point out errors but in a way that left the recipient feeling they had been advised, never chastised. I, and I know a lot of others, will miss him.

Kevin Robertson

# Introduction

**We like curios and this is certainly one. Of course somebody out there will say, 'Oh that is so and so...', well if that is you, do please share it with us. Something in the depths of the mind is recalling Nine Elms goods and the 'shunt signal' is certainly similar to one seen at Midhurst LSW on p87 of Vol 1 of 'Southern Infrastructure'. Any information is very welcome.**

# The Kent Coal Industry
## John Perkin

## Introduction

After I completed my Student Engineering Apprenticeship with the Yorkshire Electricity Board, I was head-hunted by the South Eastern Electricity Board and moved to their East Kent District in St. Peters, Broadstairs. Whenever I move to a new area, I endeavour to research the local history and thus became aware of Chislet Colliery and the failed Wingham Colliery in my new area.

For two years I was seconded to the head office in Hove, East Sussex, but later I was posted to the new South Kent District based in Folkestone. Our area included the East Kent Railway and the working collieries at Betteshanger, Tilmanstone and Snowdown. When passing during my duties I often stopped for a few minutes to watch steam locomotives in operation at Betteshanger. Arriving five years too late to see steam on the local main lines, it was a revelation to see steam operations in Kent.

## The discovery of coal in Kent

Geologists first speculated that there was coal beneath Kent in the 1840s. It was not until the latter part of the nineteenth century, however, that the theory was properly investigated.

In 1880, work began at Dover's Shakespeare Cliff on a Channel Tunnel from Dover to Calais. The idea of a Channel Tunnel had been discussed for some time but always with trepidation, the fear being the Tunnel could compromise national security; indeed, in 1882 the government halted the Channel Tunnel work while it considered the military implications. (The 'Entente Cordiale' which was subsequently signed on 8 April 1904 was a major step in improving the relations between Britain and France.)

The colliery at Shakespeare Cliff, operational between 1905 and 1915 during which time it produced just 1,000 tons output. Although not specifically referred to, there may even have been periods when it was temporarily mothballed – perhaps the photograph was taken during one of these times as there would appear to be little obvious activity. The main line between Folkestone and Dover may be seen passing to the right.

Meanwhile, back in the 1880s and with its workers lying idle, the Channel Tunnel Company decided to drill bore holes to investigate Kent's geology. The result was the discovery of both iron ore and coal in 1890.

Shareholders of the Channel Tunnel Company declined to allow the Company to exploit the coal. The mineral rights instead went to Arthur Burr, who set up the Kent Coalfields Syndicate in 1896. Burr then proceeded to set up Shakespeare Colliery at the old tunnel workings. This was operational between 1905 – 1915 and had a rail connection from the Folkestone to Dover main line. The total output was just 1,000 tons.

Coal had been discovered at a depth of 300 metres (980ft) below Shakespeare Cliff on 15 February 1890. The first shaft was started on 21 August 1891 and had cast iron tubes added as the shaft was sunk. The first coal seam was hit on 25 September 1903.

Unfortunately by February 1905 only 12 tons of coal had been brought to the surface, although curiously in 1907 a brewery in Dover purchased the first commercial coal from the pit and advertised their product 'Dover Pale Ale' as 'Brewed by Kent Coal'.

With limited success at coal extraction it was not surprising that the colliery closed in 1909 and the company was placed in the hands of the receiver. But it was not the end as work commenced again in 1910 and there was even a small stopping place opened on the main line nearby; Shakespeare Cliff Halt opening in 1913 to serve the miners. The colliery finally closed in December 1915 due to geological problems, with the equipment sold for scrap in 1918. The site has been since obliterated by workings in connection with building the Channel Tunnel.

By definition the Kent Coalfield encompassed an area located in the eastern part of the county. The Coalfields Trust defines the Kent Coalfield as in the wards of Barnham Downs and Marshside in the Canterbury district, and the wards of Aylesham, Eastry, Eythorne and Shepherdswell, Middle Deal and Sholden, Mill Hill and North Deal in the Dover district.

Notwithstanding the limited success being enjoyed at Shakespeare, in 1911 a serious investigation began into the amount of coal that might exist elsewhere within the eastern part of the county. Six 'bore holes' were put down in search of coal (the locations were Rushbourne, Hoads Wood, in Sturry, Herne Bay, Reculver, Chitty (which is near Chislet) and Chislet Park – which was near the future site of Hersden). In those early years many collieries were sunk but failed, although the East Kent Light Railway was built to exploit the anticipated business. Kent coal was some of the most difficult coal to extract and consequently it was also some of the most expensive in Britain. The whole industry was always close to failing for the first fifty years of its operation and came close to being abandoned on numerous occasions.

Several Kent coalfields did survive and in common with the coal industry elsewhere were nationalised in 1947. This was to be a brief renaissance for as early as 1960 the then National Coal Board commenced plans to start closing the Kent collieries.

As mentioned, extensive plans had been drawn up by 1914 for major coal exploitation in east Kent, and the coalfield expanded rapidly in the late 1920s and early 1930s, with its maximum output reached around 1936. (1935 figures show that the total output for the year was 2,089,205 tons, equivalent to 284 tonnes per operative.) Unfortunately the outbreak of war and disappointing test results at some drillings eventually resulted in only four collieries surviving: Betteshanger, Chislet, Snowdown and Tilmanstone. Had coal been more easily accessible, the open, rural landscape of east Kent could have changed beyond recognition.

## Geology

Various geologists, including Robert Godwin-Austen, had theorised that the geological conditions in East Kent were conducive to the existence of coal and therefore the potential for coal mining. Godwin-Austen put forward his views in 1857, and they were accepted by Sir Joseph Prestwich, who was a member of the Royal Coal Commission from 1866–1871.

The rock sequences found within the concealed coalfields of Kent, Berkshire and Oxfordshire have been formally renamed in recent years using terms established for the South Wales Coalfield. Much of the strata now assigned to the Warwickshire Group was formerly assigned to the Upper Coal Measures.

## The Collieries

**Betteshanger.** Pearson & Dorman Long Ltd built a railway line to the site of their new Colliery, with sidings at the end of the branch which ran north-west from a junction on the Dover-Sandwich line; the colliery was operational from 1924 to 1989.

The branch was later cut back to a rapid-loading pad, half a mile from the main line, and the use of NCB locos ceased in 1976. Narrow gauge locos were used underground, but not on the surface.

Despite considerable investment in surface and underground modernisation in 1951-54, costs increased and production dropped, halving to only 348,000 tons in 1958 although further investment in the 1960s saw that increase to over 500,000 tons.

Betteshanger miners were regarded as the most militant in Kent and this was also the only pit to strike during WW2. (This came about in consequence of the July 1940 legislation allowing the Minister of Labour to ban strikes and lockouts, and force compulsory arbitration. Order 1305 allowed the Minister to refer any dispute to existing arbitration structures or the National Arbitration Tribunal – either alternative was to be binding. Even so, on 9 January 1942 miners at Betteshanger struck over the level of allowances for working difficult seams. The Ministry of Labour decided to prosecute 1,050 miners for contravening Order 1305. Three local union officials were imprisoned, the men working difficult seams were fined £3 each, and 1,000 other miners were fined £1 each. Betteshanger continued their strike and other pits came out in sympathy. On 28 January they won, and in February the Home Secretary dropped the prison sentences. By May, only nine miners had paid their fines. Most of the fines were never paid.)

Betteshanger Colliery was also the largest colliery in Kent, but never developed its full potential. The loss of the local Richborough Power Station market, converted from coal to oil in 1971, had a major impact on operations. It was also the last colliery to return to work following the 1984/85 miners' strike and eventually closed on 26 August 1989.

**Two steam engines from different eras at Betteshanger on 23 May 1959. Leading is *St Martin* built in 1931 by the Avonside Company and at the rear 'Austerity' No 9 dating from 1954 and a Hunslet. The pair were photographed on 23 May 1959.** *R. C. Riley/Transport Treasury collection*

# The Kent Coal Industry

## Maximum outputs

Pre-War – 883,498 tonnes in 1935, 355 tonnes per operative.
Post-War – 610,000 tonnes in 1951, 304 tonnes per operative.
Final – 345,383 tonnes in 1987/88, 603 tonnes per operative.

Locomotives used at varying times during the period of operation, all standard gauge:

|  | Builder/Wks. | No. | Date |
| --- | --- | --- | --- |
| *St. Alpheg* | 0-6-0T OC HC | 1344 | 1918 |
| *St Edmund* | 0-6-0T OC HC | 1345 | 1918 |
| 1 *St. Augustine* | 0-6-0ST IC HC | 1495 | 1923 |
| *St Martin* | 0-6-0ST OC AE | 2064 | 1931 |
| No9 | 0-6-0ST IC HE | 3825 | 1954 |
| No10 | 0-6-0ST IC HE | 3827 | 1954 |
| 31556 | 0-6-0T IC Afd |  | 1909 |
| No11 | 0-6-0ST OC YE | 2440 | 1948 |
| DS235 (30066) | 0-6-0T OC VIW | 4377 | 1942 |
| 30068 | 0-6-0T OC VIW | 4444 | 1943 |
| – | 0-4-0ST OC P | 2156 | 1955 |
| No12 *Arthur Leighton* | 0-6-0ST IC HC | 1754 | 1943 |
| 12131 No1802/B3 | 0-6-0DE Dar |  | 1952 |
| D4067 No1802/B4 | 0-6-0DE Dar |  | 1961 |
| 15224 No1802/B5 | 0-6-0DE Afd |  | 1949 |

(AE – Avonside Engine Co
Afd – Ashford
Dar – Darlington
HC – Hudswell Clarke
P – Peckett
VIW – Vulcan Iron Works
YE – Yorkshire Engine Co)

**Chislet.** Operational 1918 to 1969. Served by sidings on the north side of the Canterbury (West) – Ramsgate line, east of Chislet Colliery Halt. Despite considerable investment in the 1950s, production declined steadily, from 475,000 tons in 1955 to 346,000 tons in 1963-64.

In 1963/64 a 550V dc railway was built to the south-eastern area of the mine which had formerly used battery locomotives.

**Chislet from above around the time of closure, 1969.**

The colliery was placed in jeopardy in December 1968 and closed in 1969. It was the first Kent colliery to close with the end of main line steam in 1968 as its principal customer was for steam coal. Chislet Colliery Halt subsequently closed on 4 October 1971 and its signal box on 23 July 1984.

Locomotives used at varying times during the period of operation, all standard gauge:

|  | Builder/Wks. | No. | Date |
| --- | --- | --- | --- |
| *Chislet Colliery* | 0-4-0ST OC P | 1626 | 1924 |
| *Bessie* | 0-4-0ST OC WB | 2272 | 1925 |
| 30083 (83) | 0-4-0T OC LSW |  | 1908 |
| 86 | 0-4-0T OC LSW | 891 |  |
| 90 | 0-4-0T OC LSW |  | 1892 |
| 89 | 0-4-0T OC LSW |  | 1892 |
| 30096 | 0-4-0T OC LSW |  | 1893 |
| 82 | 0-4-0T OC LSW |  | 1908 |
| *Chislet No2* | 0-4-0ST OC WB | 2961 | 1950 |
| 1 *St. Augustine* | 0-6-0ST IC HC | 1495 | 1923 |
| 31027 | 0-6-0T IC Afd |  | 1910 |
|  | 0-4-0DM JF | 4160002 | 1952 |
|  | 0-6-0ST OC YE | 2498 | 1951 |
|  | 0-4-0ST OC P | 2156 | 1955 |
|  | 0-6-0DM AB | 382 | 1950 |

(AB – Andrew Barclay
Afd – Ashford
HC – Hudswell Clarke
JF – John Fowler
LSW – London & South Western Railway
P – Peckett
WB – William Bagnell
YE – Yorkshire Engine Co)

**Snowdown.** The colliery here had an extensive internal standard gauge rail network, connected to the Dover to Canterbury (East) main line at Snowdown and also at Nonington Halt. The colliery was operational from 1912 to 1987.

The line was operated by steam locomotives, the last of which survived in working condition after the demise of steam traction on the national main line in 1968. The colliery railway was by then using a mixed fleet of steam and diesel locomotives with the final steam withdrawals taking place in the late 1970s.

The final three steam locomotives were named after saints with nearby Canterbury connections. *St Thomas* (named for St Thomas of Canterbury), *St Dunstan* (named for Dunstan, also a medieval Archbishop of Canterbury), and *St Martin* (named for St Martin, patron of England's oldest parish church, St Martin's Church, Canterbury). *St Thomas* and *S. Dunstan* are both preserved. *St Martin* was badly damaged when its tanks were left full of water and subsequently froze, it was then scrapped.

The colliery railway network was dismantled following the closure of the colliery in 1987. Narrow gauge locos were used underground, but not on the surface.

Output was nearly 600,000 tonnes per annum between the late 1950s and early 1960s, but only 80% was saleable due to the dirt content. This had fallen to 142,000 tonnes in 1980/81. Snowdown was also the deepest mine in Kent at 3,083 feet.

*St Thomas*, another Avonside Engine Co product, this time from 1927, seen here with her (his?) crew at Snowdown on 23 May 1959. We may assume the third man may have been a shunter rather than footplate staff. Notice the man on the right has protected his legs from blowing coal dust at the ankles. *R. C. Riley/Transport Treasury collection*

*St Dunstan* from the same builder and the same year, again at Snowdown. The presence of a top lamp bracket will be noticed, possibly only used if needed for a marker light when shunting in darkness. *R. C. Riley/Transport Treasury collection*

# The Kent Coal Industry

Locomotives used at varying times during the period of operation, all standard gauge:

|  | Builder/Wks. | No. | Date |
|---|---|---|---|
| *St Thomas* | 0-6-0ST OC AE | 1971 | 1927 |
| *St Dunstan* | 0-6-0ST OC AE | 2004 | 1927 |
| 31323 | 0-6-0T IC Afd |  | 1910 |
| 30084 | 0-4-0T OC LSW |  | 1908 |
| – | 0-4-0DM JF | 4160002 | 1952 |
| No11 | 0-6-0ST OC YE | 2440 | 1948 |
| *S. Martin* | 0-6-0ST OC AE | 2064 | 1931 |
| – | 0-6-0DM AB | 382 | 1950 |
| No9 No1802/B1 | 0-6-0ST IC HE | 3825 | 1954 |
| 15224 No1802/B5 | 0-6-0DE Afd |  | 1949 |
| D4067 No1802/B4 | 0-6-0DE Dar |  | 1961 |
| 12131 No1802/B3 | 0-6-0DE Dar |  | 1952 |
| No2 NCB 8 | 4wDH TH 120C |  | 1962 |

(AB – Andrew Barclay
AE – Avonside Engine Co
Afd – Ashford
Dar – Darlington
JF – John Fowler
LSW – London & South Western Railway
P – Peckett
TH – Thomas Hill
YE – Yorkshire Engine Co)

**Tilmanstone.** The site was connected to the East Kent Light Railway in 1915 with sidings east of Eythorne station to the colliery. Operational from 1916 to 1988, with a rail connection via the East Kent Railway from the Canterbury (East) to Dover main line.

NCB standard gauge locomotives were used from 1955. Narrow gauge locos were used both underground and on the surface.

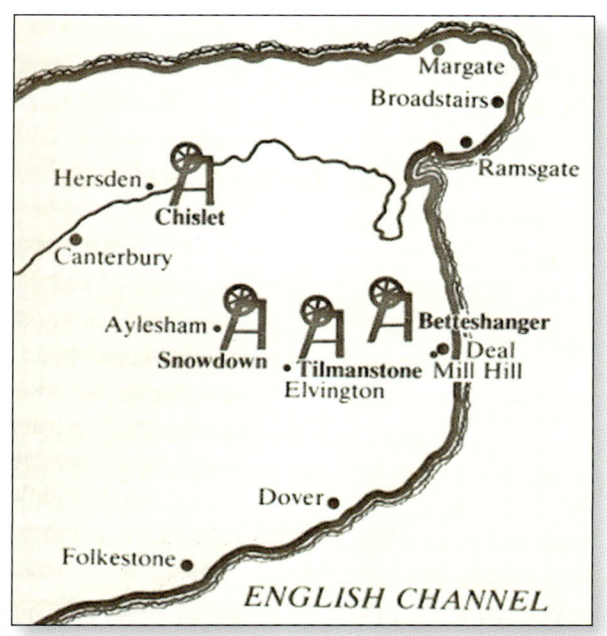

Tilmanstone was the least favoured of the Kent collieries producing less than 300,000 tons annually, although this improved slightly in the 1960s.

Locomotives used at varying times during the period of operation, all standard gauge:

|  | Builder/Wks. | No. | Date |
|---|---|---|---|
| No10 1802/B2 | 0-6-0ST IC HE | 3827 | 1954 |
| No11 | 0-4-0DM HE | 4679 | 1955 New |
| – | 0-4-0ST OC P | 2156 | 1955 |

(HE – Hunslet Engine Co
P – Peckett)

Total Output 20,000,000 tonnes

**Hunslet 0-4-0 diesel-mechanical No 11 of 1955 at Tilmanstone on 23 May 1959.** *R. C. Riley/Transport Treasury collection*

A special train organised by the Railway Enthusiasts Club from Farnborough on Saturday 23 May 1959 visited several of the collieries as well as remaining sections of the East Kent Light Railway. The tour was hauled by 'O1' No 31258 throughout and is seen here at Tilmanstone. (Further information on the tour may be found at https://www.sixbellsjunction.co.uk/50s/590523re.html ) *T. B. Owen/Hugh Davis.*

## British Railways electrification

There was 750V overhead line equipment at Betteshanger, Shepherdswell for Tilmanstone, and Snowdown for Class 71 electric locomotives. In practice these engines were not often used as mostly Class 33s and 73s operated the coal trains and the return of empties.

## Overhead ropeway from Tilmanstone to Dover Harbour

To break the East Kent Railway monopoly and to reduce transportation costs, an aerial ropeway was proposed between Tilmanstone Colliery and Dover Harbour.

Applications were made in September 1926 to Dover Corporation for the aerial ropeway, and to the Railway and Canal Commission to erect the equipment between the colliery and the Eastern Arm of the Eastern Dockyard.

A series of endless cables was supported on steel towers, with buckets attached at intervals. Each held three quarters of a ton of coal, and took one hour 45 minutes to travel from the mine to the bunker. Where the ropeway crossed roads there was a bridge of the girder or suspension type.

To avoid high winds at the Dover Cliff edge, a twin tunnel through the cliff at Dover delivered the coal to a 5,000 ton bunker at the harbour. The tunnel came out directly above the Eastern Arm about halfway down the cliff.

The proposed cost given was £61,195 and the application stated that the aerial ropeway would be carried on poles or standards of steel or ferro-concrete about 120 yards apart.

The costs, though, were somewhat underestimated and the ropeway eventually cost £125,000 with an additional £25,000 for the coal staithe. The first part of the ropeway was in use by October 1929, and all was officially opened on 14 February 1930.

It was capable of carrying 3,000 tons of coal a day at a cost at the time of opening of 1s 9d per ton against 5s 9d by rail. Ironically the carrying capacity of the ropeway was greater than the average daily output of the colliery, which was around 1,000 tons of coal a day in 1929.

When first opened the aerial ropeway lived up to expectations except at the staithe, which quickly proved to be dangerous for the three-man team working there with one fatal accident and several injuries.

Besides carrying coal from Tilmanstone to the Eastern Arm, the ropeway was leased to other companies to carry waste minerals from the mine to a railway siding for transportation by rail to Durham where it was used in the manufacture of firebricks. Despite the potentially promising start it was little used after 1935 and had become derelict by the start of WW2.

As part of property assets at the time of nationalisation, the aerial ropeway was transferred to the Dover Harbour Board but was considered uneconomic to repair and in the early 1950s it was dismantled and removed.

## Failed Collieries with rail connections

Following the discovery of coal in Kent in 1890, there were initial predictions of at least 20 pits in Kent, but only the four featured above and the unsuccessful short-lived Shakespeare Colliery produced coal.

**Guilford** Colliery was started by Arthur Burr's Foncage Syndicate (he with the Shakespeare connection). The first test shaft was sunk in 1906 hoping to find the coal seams discovered under Waldershare Park but instead of coal it was water that was discovered at a depth of 1,346ft. The East Kent Light Railway was connected to the colliery in November 1912. Still no coal had been found by 1918 and the colliery closed in the 1920s owing to geological problems.

Hammill, Woodnesborough. This site, located to the south of Woodnesborough, was also known as Hammill Colliery and was served by a half mile branch from the East Kent Light Railway. Two shafts were commenced in 1910, but were abandoned in 1914 without coal being found and the site was mothballed.

Wingham Colliery was commenced in 1910 by Burr's Wingham & Stour Valley Collieries Ltd. The colliery was to be served by the East Kent Light Railway.

Surface buildings were erected and two shafts were dug, but when water was hit there was not enough finance to buy and install pumps. It was abandoned in 1914 without any coal being found, the buildings though were left and eventually sold in 1924 to a milling business.

## The East Kent Railway

The first section of line left the former SECR Canterbury – Dover route at Shepherdswell and proceeded north through Golgotha Tunnel and cutting, by far the biggest engineering works on the line, to a junction at Eythorne with a branch to Tilmanstone. This was open by the end of 1911.

By the autumn of the following year the line had reached Eastry and by the end of the year had branched west to reach Wingham Colliery. But now instead of heading directly for the originally intended Richborough the plans were changed to extend the line to Canterbury. Like many ambitious railway schemes this was, however, never achieved, the line terminating 'in a field' at Wingham, Canterbury Road.

Meanwhile a massive military port was being constructed to the north at Richborough as part of the war effort and the EKR already had authority to construct a line there. This opened to goods traffic at the end of 1916 but after the war Richborough ceased to be a great port and traffic declined sharply.

The overhead cableway emerges from the twin tunnels at Dover Eastern Docks. Subsequent upon the abandonment of the cableway and removal of the equipment, the tunnels were sealed.

The East Kent Railway.

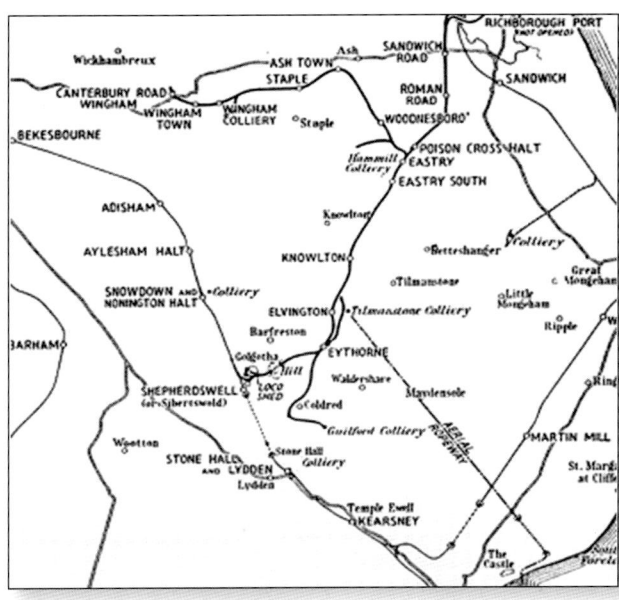

Permission to run passenger trains to Richborough had originally been refused due to weak bridges over the River Stour and the SR main line but in an effort to offset dwindling receipts, passenger trains were run on the Richborough branch from the end of 1925 but only as far as Sandwich Road. This venture was an economic failure and the service was withdrawn in the autumn of 1928. Although Richborough had become an important port during WWI, the line did not cross the River Stour until after the war, by which time the port was in decline. Branch lines to Canterbury, Deal and Birchington were planned, but never completed.

For the rest of its existence the EKR struggled along with meagre agricultural traffic, a very limited passenger revenue and its mainstay; the coal traffic over the short distance from Tilmanstone to Shepherdswell. The line was nationalised in 1948, much to the relief of its shareholders who got compensation, and the remaining passenger services were withdrawn on 1 November of that year.

The railway had been built to light railway standards by its engineer, Colonel H .F. Stephens. The first passengers were carried in 1916, with just a few facilities being provided for them. Passenger services between Eastry and Sandwich Road halts were withdrawn on 31 October 1928. When the railways were nationalised, the route became part of the Southern Region and all passenger services were completely withdrawn on 1 November 1948.

However, the line from Shepherdswell to Tilmanstone Colliery remained operational until the 1984/85 Miners' Strike. Tilmanstone Colliery reopened for a short while, but eventually ceased production in October 1986. Closure of the line followed in 1987.

All traffic north of Eythorne ceased on 1 March 1951, traffic to Wingham, Canterbury Road having already ceased on 25 July the previous year (the line still presumably being maintained). Coal continued to be transported from Tilmanstone to the junction with the SECR at Shepherdswell until April 1984.

## Preservation

In November 1985, the East Kent Railway Society was formed with the intention of saving and reopening the remaining line, but it was not until 1989 that volunteers were able to start the massive task of clearing the tangle of shrubs, trees and other vegetation that had claimed the railway since closure. The EKRS has since transformed the station area and its environs at Shepherdswell, with a replica of the original station building and platform being built, along with new access roads, car parks laid, and the addition of toilet blocks, a café and picnic areas.

In 1993, their Light Railway Order was obtained, allowing regular passenger trains to run on the East Kent Railway, after an absence of over forty years. Since then a new station has been built at Eythorne. In 2003 the East Kent Railway also became a Charitable Trust.

## Conclusions

The Kent Coal Industry existed for over seventy years and internal and main line railways played a significant part in the extraction and distribution of coal. Simply put it was loss of markets, difficult geology, politics and climate change that brought about its eventual end.

## References:

'The East Kent Light Railway', A.R.Catt, published The Oakwood Press, 1970.

'The East Kent Light Railway', Vic Mitchell & Keith Smith, published Middleton Press, 1989.

'The East Kent Railway' Volumes 1 & 2, Lawson-Finch and Garrett, published The Oakwood Press, 2003.

## Acknowledgments:

Darran Cowd, Betteshanger Sustainable Parks.

Robin Waywell, Industrial Railway Society, with many thanks for the locomotive histories.

Members of the SEMG Yahoo Group.

At the former Betteshanger Colliery site the Kent Mining Museum is being built and was scheduled to open at the end of March 2019. Their website is:

www.betteshanger-park.co.uk/kent-mining-museum/

The museum will focus on the four main colliery sites in Kent, Chislet, Betteshanger, Snowdown and Tilmanstone.

# Nostalgia at Portsmouth

## Sean Bolan

**Portsmouth & Southsea 1951. No names or other information – just good old fashioned nostalgia.**

The name Sean Bolan will likely be familiar to many. In the opinion of the editor Sean is one of the finest railway painters active today, being able to identify a worthwhile subject for his talents and, away from painting, to similarly identify a great photograph when it appears. Sean's work has graced the cover (and pages) of many a railway tome, including our own 'Basingstoke & Alton Light Railway', and 'Meon Valley Part 3'. A recent visit to Sean at his rural Cotswold home also elicited the following comment, '....came across these recently, thought you might be interested....' Well we certainly are, a delightful selection of Portsmouth Town in 1951 recording a railway era probably recalled by many readers of SW but now totally swept away – dingy corners, dusty platforms, indeed almost a feeling of continuing austerity. Perhaps we should be more appreciative of modernisation after all!

There appears to have been neither rhyme nor reason as to where the photographer pointed his camera at Portsmouth and these are just a selection from double the number available, all taken, it seems, around the same time and in the same area. Readers will no doubt find their own area of nostalgia in the selection, whether that be the notices, people and dress, or just the general ambiance of the railway 60+ years ago. If it looks drab, let us be honest and acknowledge it was, but no different to countless other stations, not just on the Southern. In many respects it was surprising it even survived considering the pounding Portsmouth had received in WW2. To the present writer some things especially stick in the mind; the grey and

# Nostalgia at Portsmouth

invariably dusty platform surface, the aroma of paraffin and Jeyes fluid seemingly around every corner and those wooden benches. In some respects almost like a garden seat and which, if another person deemed to sit down, would adjust themselves accordingly. It was not a good idea to linger too long and from a comfort perspective they certainly did not encourage it. (There's more to come in another issue as well as a few similar images of Brighton at around the same time.)

# Victorian Boom and Bust
## Railway Mania and the Bank of Overend Gurney

### John Burgess

Dating back to 1830, *Invicta* has a number of claims to fame; built by Messrs Robert Stephenson, she was the final engine built to what could rightly be called the 'first phase' of locomotive design which had started back in 1802 with 'Pen-y-Darren' by Trevithick. *Invicta* was also built immediately after the famed *Rocket*. (Subsequent to *Invicta*, Stephenson produced *Planet*, which basic design was to form the basis of the modern steam locomotive.) *Invicta* also hauled the first locomotive-hauled passenger train on the Canterbury and Whitstable Railway and remained in service until 1839. The company then attempted to sell her but were not successful and she was stored, subsequently becoming the property of the SER when it took over the C&W. Soon after she was moved to Ashford for preservation thus becoming another first – the first locomotive to be so honoured. Following display at Canterbury the locomotive was latterly on display at the Canterbury Heritage Museum until this closed in 2017. Whilst we can be assured the fate of this historic relic is secure, its long term placing does not appear to be confirmed.

# The project

For some time I have felt that it ought to be possible to trace the effect of the trade cycle on railway construction by plotting the opening dates of lines against their route mileages. I had enough information to be able to use the constituent pre-grouping companies of the Southern Railway, having an extensive personal library supplemented with internet sources. I was expecting particularly to see evidence of the period known as the Railway Mania during the mid-1840s when railway projects reached a peak, and of the impact of the banking crisis of 1866, when the collapse of Overend Gurney set off a major economic recession. I thought that this would be quite a simple, basic research project, but it turned out that pulling all the information together would be quite a challenge, particularly in the densely developed suburban networks around London. As the project emerged, a certain amount of simplification had to be applied. For instance, mileages were rounded to the nearest half mile; most short spurs were not included; the widening of lines has been completely left out of the analysis. So the results are perhaps a little approximate; but they do correlate well with what I know about the Victorian economy.

As it usually took a year or two for lines to be constructed, I expected to find that the peak years for openings would follow the market but about two years later. So for example the Railway Mania was particularly evident in Parliament in 1845, peaking in 1846, but because of the time taken for construction, the peak year for openings was 1847.

I also expected to see a tailing off of construction after about 1880 as the network approached completion. This is generally the case, although I was quite surprised to see how much construction took place after 1890. I also expected to find that the earlier lines would generally survive closure, and the later lines would usually have disappeared from today's network. Although this is true in the broadest sense, a surprising number of late-constructed lines still survive, whilst some of the earliest lines have long disappeared. Several late lines followed the growth of the suburbs, particularly around London, and these have, by and large, survived. My rule of thumb that railways built before 1850 form the core of the present day network, whilst later lines have disappeared, does not entirely hold true.

This might seem to be a very dry subject to research, full of history and economics, but I found plenty of drama and some extremely interesting twists, particularly as a result of the 1866 crisis; railway companies and contractors failing or brought to their knees; railway promoters struggling against the odds to build lines with limited or non-existent finance; abandoned and half completed projects. Perhaps it's not quite in the mainstream, but hopefully you too will catch some of the drama.

# The trade cycle

Throughout my working life as a surveyor, the impact of the trade cycle on commercial life has fascinated me. Between 1976 and 2009 I experienced the impact of three recessions, all with different causes, but none so dramatic as that resulting from the banking crisis of 2008, when several seemingly rock-solid financial institutions came crashing down, and only the major intervention of government to shore up some of our big High Street banks prevented further failures. For a period of time I was checking daily to find out what the latest revelations were. It was certainly dramatic and at times very scary. Eleven years after these momentous events we are still feeling the after effects, as what had been a banking crisis was turned into a public finance crisis as a result of the transfer of staggering amounts of public money to save the worst cases. I expect we all remember the proud boast of a certain politician just before the crisis that 'the days of boom and bust are over'. Hmm. And of course, the banking crisis was worldwide (particularly in Europe and North America) and far more extensive than just the British cases that are more familiar to us.

There is nothing particularly new about the trade cycle, as spectacular and sometimes bizarre historical instances demonstrate. One of the oddest has to be the strange market that developed in the 1630s in Dutch tulip bulbs, when prices reached astronomical heights before a crash in 1637. In the following century the South Sea Bubble of 1720 ruined many who dabbled in the shares of the company, when the prospects of any significant trade being developed by the company were remote.

The impact of the South Sea Bubble was long lasting, as Parliament passed legislation that effectively prevented the creation of Joint Stock Companies without the company concerned obtaining its own Act of Parliament. This legislation was not repealed until 1825, and it meant that most businesses were family owned or run by private partnerships. There was no protection from any liabilities that such businesses might incur, so financial failure could bring personal ruin and, potentially, imprisonment. With the amount of finance required to develop the early railways and industrial enterprise, the repeal of the Act was essential to enable private funds to be invested. Its repeal was very much in accordance with 19th century thinking on free trade and market economics, prevalent from the 1830s onwards.

# The procedure for railway development

In broad terms, Victorian railway promoters had to obtain parliamentary approval for each public railway line, requiring the submission to Westminster of a proposal and surveyed plans of the route before any work could be commenced. The law conferred on authorised schemes compulsory purchase powers to enable the necessary land to be acquired from private owners, thereby precluding land owners from holding railway companies to ransom. The legislation gave rise to the surveying profession, and ultimately the formation of the Royal Institution of Chartered Surveyors, and practitioners today are still expected to be conversant with the process of compulsory purchase.

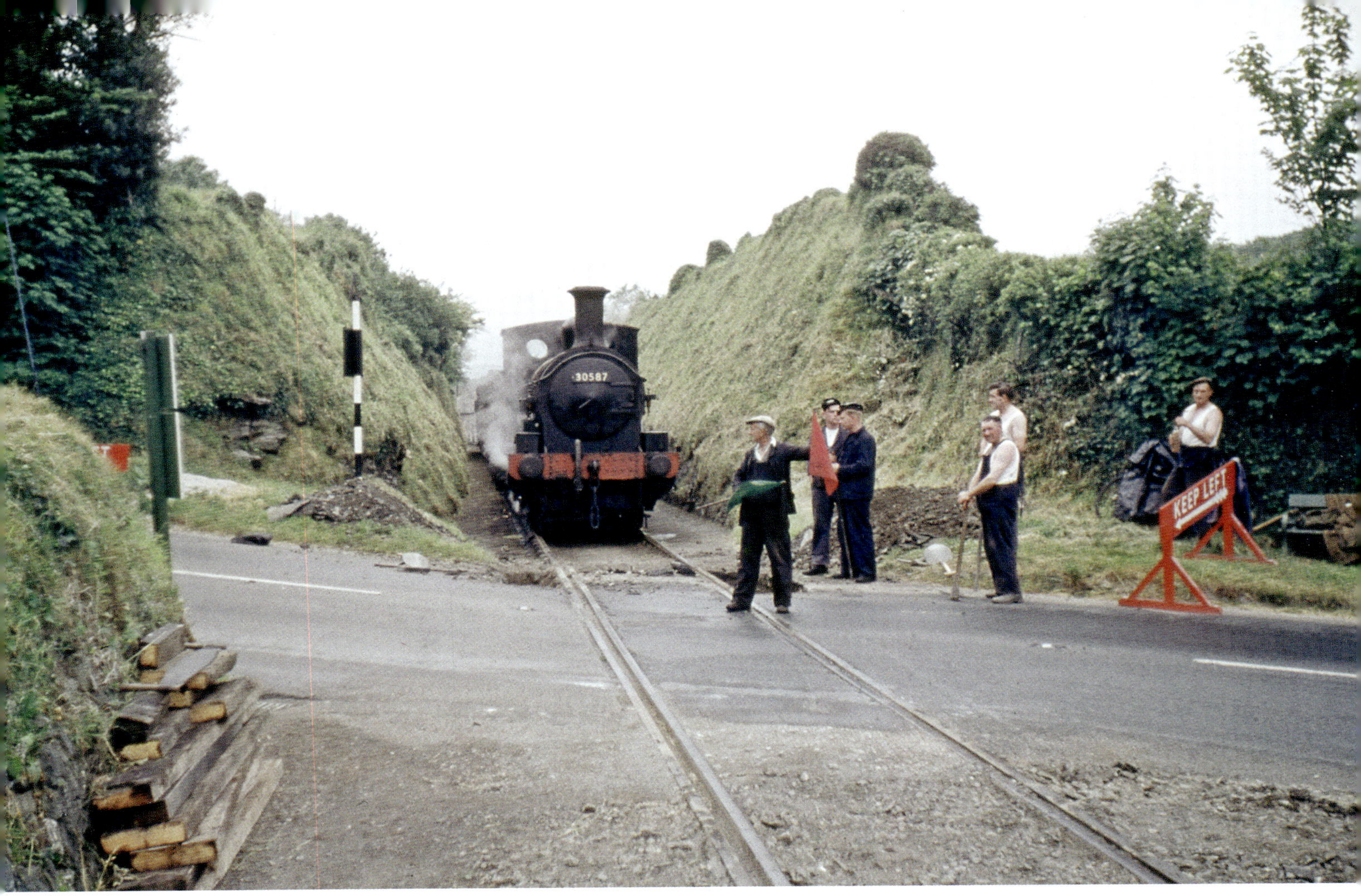
30587
KEEP LEFT

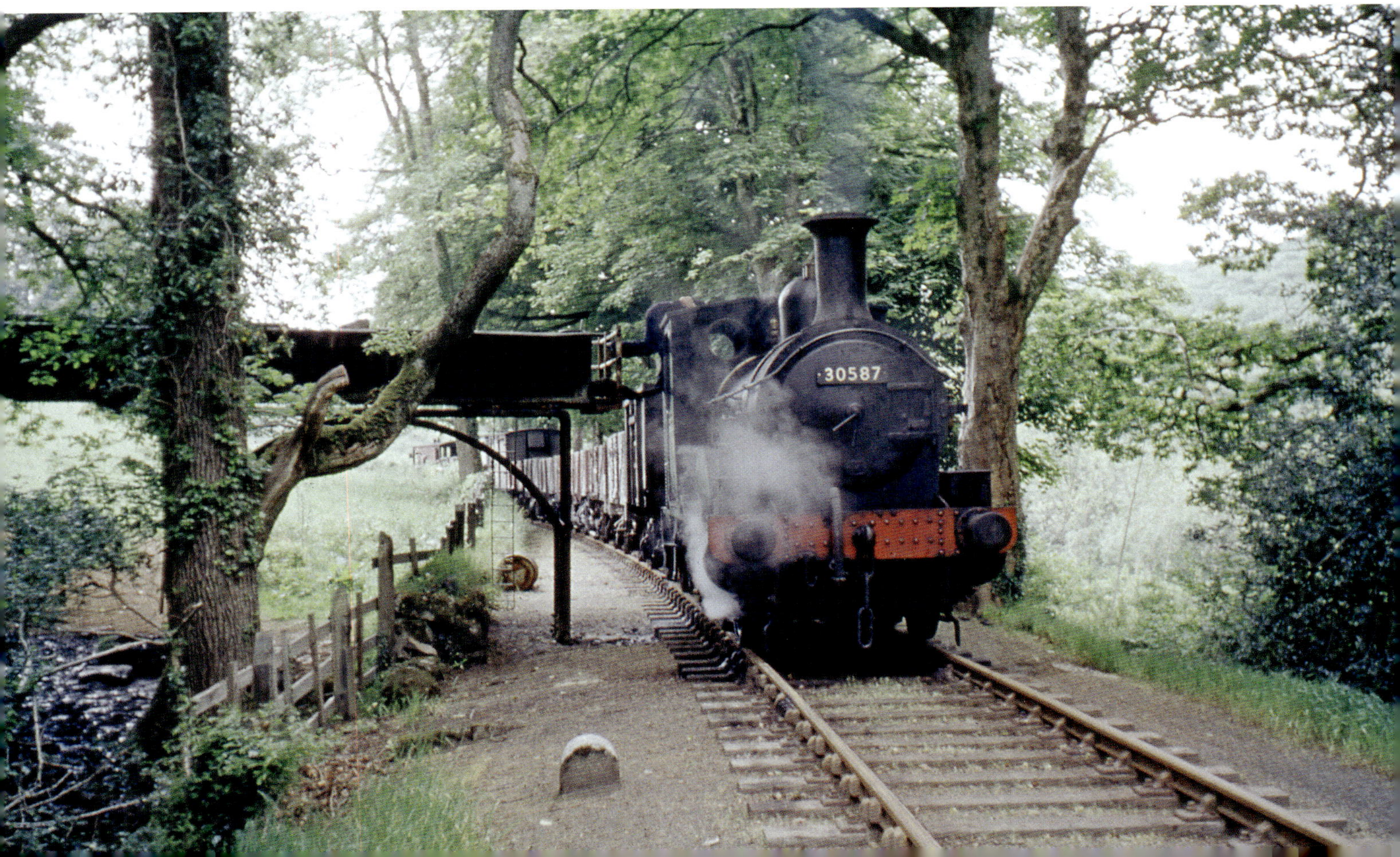
30587

Railway surveyors would be engaged to produce survey drawings (sometimes in the teeth of violent opposition from landowners who took steps forcibly to prevent the unfortunate individuals from gaining access to their estates), and thereafter to secure the purchase of land prior to construction. The cat and mouse games played by the early railway surveyors to complete their surveys and outwit landowners can make for entertaining reading. Sometimes arrangements were made to complete the survey under cover of darkness; on other occasions armed gangs confronted each other. Under these circumstances, how accurate were these surveys?

Notwithstanding this, the processes appeared to be much simpler than is the case today, with little to stand in the way of development once the all-important Act of Parliament had been secured. Today, lengthy planning processes, public enquiries and possible judicial review can extend the development process for major projects by years, even decades, and then lengthy procurement arrangements are also likely to delay start dates. By contrast, in most cases, Victorian contractors would be on site just a few weeks after parliamentary approval, with land acquisition substantially resolved, the terms probably more or less agreed prior to parliamentary approval, transactions completed soon after the granting of the all-important Act.

## Pioneer railways and the first main lines

All this sets the scene for the pioneer railways. The first railways which eventually constituted the Southern Railway were developed in the 1830s, and they make a curious selection. In Kent, the six miles of the Canterbury & Whitstable were opened in May 1830, eventually being absorbed into the South Eastern Railway. Then in far-away Cornwall, the Bodmin & Wadebridge opened on 30 September 1834 with a 7 mile line between the two towns and a 6.5 mile freight only branch to Wenford Bridge. The third early pioneer was the London & Greenwich, running for four miles from London Bridge to Greenwich and part opened on 8 February 1836, the rest of the line following later that same year. It was built on a brick viaduct of 878 arches and unlike the other two it is still open, having carried passengers now for over 180 years.

In the mid to late 1830s there was something of a boom in railway promotion when the origins of what later became the London and South Western (LSWR), the London, Brighton and South Coast (LBSC) and the South Eastern railways (SER) were all established. The main line from Nine Elms to Southampton was progressively opened between 23 May 1838 and 11 May 1840; the line from London Bridge to Brighton opened between 5 June 1839 (the London and Croydon) and 21 September 1841; and the SER main line from London Bridge to Dover via Redhill between 12 July 1841 (to Redhill) and 7 February 1844 (the final link to Dover). A short-lived atmospheric line was developed after the original Croydon Railway in 1845, and ran alongside it south of Forest Hill until it branched off to West Croydon. However, it was beset with problems and was converted to conventional haulage after two years, the LBSC inheriting a large amount of redundant pipework and equipment, the only interest in it coming from scrap dealers.

The sharing of LBSC and SER routes from London to Redhill was brought about as a result of Parliamentary insistence that only one route out of London to the south would be necessary. It ruled that the Brighton company should build the line from Coulsdon to Redhill which would be sold to the SER at cost price with the Brighton having running powers. The SER was intending to build a separate line from Croydon via Oxted, but this now had to wait until a future date. In the longer term the sharing arrangements suited neither company. This was a rare example of government interference, soon to disappear in the *laissez faire* approach to railway construction that predominated during the 19th century. With the benefit of hindsight it was not the most enlightened decision made by government.

## Railway mania

Once these first main lines were built, there was a brief lull with a few branches added (Brighton to Shoreham in 1840; Eastleigh to Gosport in 1841; Paddock Wood to Maidstone in 1844; and Woking to Guildford in 1845). However, the period known as the Railway Mania was about to burst upon us. Favourable conditions for investing in shares pertained in 1845 and 1846, and the early main lines, were earning dividends up to 10% which encouraged small investors to put their money into a host of new railway schemes. In just those two years, Parliament was besieged by railway promoters anxious to obtain approval for schemes across the country. Some were well founded, some much more speculative, some with virtually no chance of being constructed. Across the whole country, 248 schemes were presented to the 1845 parliamentary session, rising to a peak of 815 schemes in 1846. Quite how Parliament managed to give proper consideration to this number of schemes is hard to envisage; it is unlikely that any in-depth scrutiny could have been given to individual proposals, and Members of Parliament were themselves investing in the market, so were not necessarily impartial. To assist with the process, Parliament appointed a small Committee under the chairmanship of Lord Dalhousie to scrutinise proposals and determine which had no realistic prospect of progressing. The Committee was known as the 'Five Kings' and they were also asked to give some policy guidance in order to shape railway development, and to look at the problems of the gauge war. As we know, at an early date (1846), the broad gauge was discouraged but the GWR persisted with it until the 1890s.

*Opposite top:* **'Well Tank' No 30587 at Dunmere level crossing with p/way gang and flagman.** *Roger Holmes*

*Bottom:* **The same engine at the water column in the woods. Famed as running on the Bodmin and Wadebridge railway for 67 years until 1962, the Beattie 'Well Tanks' were ideal for china clay trains on what was a sharply curved railway and associated industrial sidings. Two of the three survived scrapping, No 30587 being one of them. It is seen here at the water stop in Pencarrow woods on 22 July 1960. The water filler was accessed within the bunker.** *Roger Holmes*

Some of the early entrepreneurs active at this time were not exactly scrupulous in their financial management, massaging returns by hiding unwelcome revenue expenditure in the capital account, and paying share dividends from capital, all designed to boost the value of shareholdings. Probably the most notorious of these characters was George Hudson, whose various railway companies ran from Bristol to the Midlands, and from there northwards to York (where he lived, rising to fame and then notoriety) and onwards into the North-East. His financial shenanigans were not uncovered until the late 1840s, when his unlawful and fraudulent activities were exposed and some of his railway companies more or less ruined as a result. Hudson himself disappeared overseas to avoid a potential prison sentence. Although Hudson played no part in the development of railways in the south, his influence and activity during the Mania cannot be ignored.

As news of his misdemeanours spread, potential investors became wary, and others became disillusioned as their investments disappeared into failed schemes. Railway companies experienced difficulties in securing funds, as shares were sold on a deposit basis, typically only 10% being required to secure a shareholding, with the balance being called upon as construction proceeded. However, in their eagerness to acquire shares, investors failed to keep sufficient funds available to meet these calls (arising perhaps eighteen months after the initial sale) as they overextended themselves in the frenzy. Railway companies then ran into trouble paying their contractors, and frequently contractors would have to accept payment in shares (this occurred regularly throughout the railway building years). By 1847, the risks for ordinary investors were becoming apparent. Buying shares was not a licence to print money. The rate of promotion of new schemes slowed as the markets fell. Poorly conceived schemes and duplicating lines began to fade away, leaving their investors with nothing.

The boom also created major stress in the labour market and supplying industries, the demands pushing up wages and prices. A new workforce of railway navvies developed, drawing particularly on agricultural labourers and Irish emigrants escaping the effects of famine (roughly one third were Irish). At the peak, about 250,000 were working as navvies across Britain as a whole. Unable to compete with wages offered by the railway contractors, agriculture in particular suffered from labour shortages, a driver for mechanisation of farming.

In total, Parliament authorised the construction of 8,592 route miles of railway in the three parliamentary sessions of 1845, 1846 and 1847, but of that number some 5,560 miles were abandoned or failed to progress. This brief period resulted in the construction of many useful lines, most still in use today. Of the lines destined to form the Southern Railway, the peak years for development followed the Mania years, there being typically a two or three year gap from authorisation to opening. 1846 through to 1849 saw the opening of 92.5 miles, 132.5 miles, 42.5 miles and 92 miles respectively. The 1847 figure was never surpassed, although 1860 openings came close.

Lines opened during this period included Croydon – Epsom; Shoreham – Portsmouth; Brighton and Keymer Junction – Lewes – Hastings; Polegate – Eastbourne (LBSC); Ashford – Ramsgate

Excavated pipes from the ill-fated London and Croydon atmospheric railway system, in use from around 1844 to just 1847 and which involved the laying of an additional line alongside the existing conventional railway. Three pumping stations were built but these were later demolished, although stone from one at Croydon was recycled for the construction of the Surrey Street waterworks building. The pipes seen here were no doubt removed for scrap.

– Margate; Redhill – Reading; Lewisham – Strood; Minster – Deal (SER except for Shalford Junction to Ash Junction on the Reading branch which was built by the LSWR with SER running powers); Southampton – Dorchester via Ringwood; Nine Elms – Waterloo; Clapham Junction – Richmond – Windsor; Guildford – Godalming; Eastleigh – Salisbury; Crediton – Cowley Bridge; and Fareham – Portcreek Junction (LSWR).

As evidenced by this list, the network of lines was well developed by the end of 1849. Very few lines opened before 1850 have since been closed, and where this has happened it is often the result of demographic change (such as the growth of Bournemouth in the 1880s leading to the downgrading and closure of the line through Wimborne), or later network improvements adversely impacting on some earlier lines (for example, the LSWR Portsmouth direct line reducing traffic over the branch to Gosport). It was possible to travel from Dover, Deal, Ramsgate or Margate as far west as Dorchester or Salisbury by train. To get further west, it would be necessary to travel over the broad gauge GWR from Paddington or Reading.

## Post-mania construction

After the Mania, railway development continued into the 1850s and early 1860s at a less frenetic pace as the industry began to mature and the main companies became established. The railway companies that successfully emerged from the late 1840s were now looking to establish their own networks, as far as possible excluding any competition from their rivals. The backing of an established company would give independent promoters a significant advantage and enhance their chances of success.

The situation west of Salisbury (stretching down to Exeter, and beyond, deeper into Devon and Cornwall) presents an interesting example of Victorian no-holds-barred competition. The LSWR had longstanding ambitions to get into the West Country, and a first statement of intent was its acquisition of the troubled Bodmin & Wadebridge in 1845, even though it possessed no other line nearer than Salisbury at the time. In this respect, it was at a great disadvantage compared with the GWR and the Bristol & Exeter which had opened its broad gauge main line as far as Exeter in 1844, extended to Plymouth by the South Devon in 1848, and then into Cornwall as far as Truro in 1859 (this through the Cornwall and West Cornwall Railways).

The LSWR had to act fast, as the broad gauge was being pushed west to Crediton, and later to Barnstaple and Bideford by the Exeter & Crediton and the North Devon. The LSWR acquired a controlling shareholding in the E & C (illegally, but without sanctions being applied), and proceeded to delay its opening from 1847 until 1851. It then moved to acquire the NDR from under the noses of the GWR and its allies. Eventually these lines were opened (the NDR in 1854) and leased to the broad gauge operators (in the case of the NDR, this was the contractor, Thomas Brassey).

At length, the LSWR reached Exeter from Salisbury, the West Country main line opening in stages and eventually reaching Exeter Central in 1860, with a link into St Davids in the following year. The LSWR was then in a position to exploit its earlier acquisitions to Crediton, Barnstaple and Bideford, and laid in mixed gauge. Eventually, the broad gauge services came to an end, and the LSWR extended its reach to the north coast of Devon and Cornwall, but we are getting a long way ahead of the plot.

The years from 1850 to 1857 saw steady but unspectacular development of the network. We have seen that the LSWR gave priority to pressing westwards from Salisbury towards Exeter and beyond. It also took steps to develop what later became a suburban network to the south-west of London, reaching Hounslow, Wokingham, Farnham and Alton during these years. The boom years extended into the mid-1860s.

The LBSC also began to develop a complex network of suburban lines across South London, reaching Crystal Palace from three directions, West Croydon to Wimbledon, and opening a branch from Three Bridges to East Grinstead.

The SER was also active during this period, reaching Hastings from both Tunbridge Wells and Ashford, extending the Maidstone line to Strood, reaching Caterham from Purley and Beckenham Junction from Lewisham.

The first lines on the Isle of Wight were built towards the end of this boom period. The Cowes and Newport opened in 1862, followed by the Isle of Wight Railway from Ryde to Shanklin in 1864, extended to Ventnor in 1866. The IWR remained relatively financially secure, although it had to operate carefully, and money was certainly tight during the 1870s.

The Failure of Overend, Gurney and Company, and the Aftermath 1858 was a momentous year as it saw the rise of a fourth main line railway, the London, Chatham and Dover. Starting as a fairly innocuous entity between Chatham and Faversham, it soon realised ambitions to create a competing route to Dover. If the SER had been less riddled with internal divisions, it should have quickly absorbed this upstart, but the LCDR rapidly extended its line across South-East London and into Kent. By 1861 the line from Victoria to Dover was opened, with much of the rest of its lines being completed by 1865, reaching Sheerness, Margate, Ramsgate, Sevenoaks, Crystal Palace High Level and Blackfriars to Beckenham. Its main rival, the SER, opened lines from London Bridge to Charing Cross and Cannon Street, and, spurred on by the LCDR, started the cut-off from Lewisham which in 1868 was completed to Tonbridge, significantly shortening the mileage between London and Dover.

Whilst the network developed steadily during these years, with 1860 being a peak year (120.5 route miles opened), storm clouds were gathering. The bank of Overend, Gurney and Company had been established in 1800 as a wholesale discount bank buying and selling bills of exchange. It had developed an extensive business, and had moved into investing in shares, including some railway companies, encouraged by a rising market. It had become the largest such financial institution by the mid-nineteenth century. Its failure was fairly protracted, and can be traced back to an American banking crash in 1857, when Overend Gurney took advantage of its size to intervene and acquire investments (not necessarily with a great deal of prudence) but retaining insufficient liquidity to cover itself. At this time there was also a great deal of friction between the Bank of England and Overend Gurney. For instance, in 1860 Overend Gurney attempted to create a run on the Bank of England, which in the event failed to materialise, but this hardly made for good relationships. By 1866 the bank had become overstretched with liquid assets of £1 million set against liabilities of £4 million. A rapid fall in the stock market in the mid-1860s precipitated a run on the bank, and despite making efforts to recover its liquidity, it failed on 10 May 1866, and went into liquidation in June 1866. The Bank of England made no attempt to salvage the bank, but unsuccessfully invested substantial sums to support the bill market, particularly between 10 and 12 May. Railway shares were particularly badly affected by the fall in the stock market, and the knock on effects were extensive, over 200 companies failing in the aftermath, including banks, railway companies and contractors. There are some striking parallels with the 2008 banking crisis.

The well known image of Eastleigh (at the time more accurately described as 'Bishopstoke' looking north). No date, but from the attire I think we can safely say sometime in the 1806s (I assume this should be the 1860s?). Bishopstoke was the junction for the branches to Gosport and Salisbury, both lines of which still survive today. Some of the infrastructure also remains in the form of the buildings on either platform, although both bridges are totally altered.

The LCDR was particularly vulnerable to the market collapse. Its main contractor was the partnership of Peto, Betts and Crampton. Samuel Morton Peto had risen from a background as a builder, and had developed his interests in railway construction. In the 1840s he had won the contract to build the Southampton & Dorchester, and had been active in building a number of other railways including much of the Eastern Counties, later to form part of the Great Eastern. He was also active in building railways overseas, and had interests in shipping companies. On the back of his success he was able to support a lavish lifestyle and had acquired the estate at Somerleyton near Lowestoft which he redeveloped for his main residence.

By the mid-1860s Peto was already in financial trouble as a result of the poor performance of some of his investments. While the market remained buoyant he was able to continue with his business, but with the collapse he was exposed to potential bankruptcy. The LCDR had grown very rapidly, but it had cut corners in order to do so. Contracts were let to Peto, Betts and Crampton in an unlawful manner. The railway engaged the contractor without entering into competitive tendering (not illegal but poor practice) and illegally funded the contracts with debenture loans advanced by Peto at fixed interest rates, without having sold shares. (The law required a minimum proportion of shares to have been sold before debentures could be issued.) To give the impression of lawfulness, receipts were issued between the two parties implying that shares had been sold to the contractor. As the works progressed, the railway ran up debts which could not be supported from revenue, the interest charges mounting rapidly. The LCDR became insolvent in August 1866, and Peto also went bankrupt, more or less finishing him as a railway contractor.

Fortunately for the travelling public, the LCDR main line and its branches had been completed by the time of the crisis, only the branch line from Nunhead to Greenwich Park remaining incomplete. In the normal course of events, the railway would have been sold, but there were no interested parties able to acquire the LCDR after its collapse. It is known that the LBSC was interested, but the banking crisis had all but ruined this company. The SER were also not prepared to buy out the LCDR. They had taken a strangely indifferent approach to the LCDR when it first came on the scene, but with the benefit of hindsight might well have wished that they had bought out the insolvent railway when the opportunity had arisen as they were now set for three decades of crippling competition. At this time, the SER board of directors was split and ineffective, and it took the autocratic figure of Sir Edward Watkins to become Chairman and bring direction to the company. Unfortunately, much of his leadership was aimed at impoverishing the LCDR, and this adversely impacted on the SER.

An interesting casualty of the crash was the London, Lewes & Brighton, promoted as a joint venture by the SER and the LCDR, and authorised by Parliament in August 1866. It was a successor to an 1863 proposal which failed to secure parliamentary approval (the Beckenham, Lewes and Brighton Railway). The line would have run from Beckenham (where connections from London by both partners were available) to Brighton via East Grinstead, Lewes and Rottingdean with branches to Edenbridge and Westerham. Tunnelling would have been required to get through the North Downs in the Biggin Hill area. A separate Brighton terminus was proposed on the east side of Steine Gardens, the line running in through a long tunnel from the east of the town. The station here would have been much nearer to the seafront than the LBSC terminus, and likely to be attractive to day trippers and holidaymakers. Following the banking crisis, the LCDR were forced to drop out and the SER also abandoned the proposal in 1868, leaving Brighton solely in the hands of the LBSC. Had it not been for the financial crisis, there is every possibility that something close to the Bluebell Railway would have been built fifteen years earlier, and that it would not have been an LBSC branch, but a joint LCDR/SER main line competing for the Brighton traffic, a fascinating thought.

## Victorian Boom and Bust

The LCDR remained in receivership into the 1870s. In 1873, the managing director, James Staats Forbes, took over as chairman, and the company was refinanced. He ran the railway until his retirement in 1904. He was quite capable of giving the SER a bloody nose if it suited him, which very often it did.

After the crash, the LCDR built no new railway lines of any significance until 1874, when the line from Otford to Maidstone East was opened, bringing the LCDR – SER feud to another important town in Kent. In the same year, it also opened Holborn Viaduct station.

The position of the LBSC after the crisis has been touched on. In 1866, the board sought a report from their accountants (Price, Heyland and Waterhouse). The report was received in 1867 and it pointed out that during the early 1860s the railway had overextended itself financially and recommended that a number of projects should be abandoned. Some of the recently opened lines were bringing in disappointing returns, particularly the Horsham to Guildford branch (other new lines included Petworth to Midhurst, Tunbridge Wells to East Grinstead and Sutton to Epsom Downs, none of which could be considered likely to generate substantial amounts of revenue).

As a result of the report, the board took immediate steps to stop any further work on the Ouse Valley line, which was to run from south of Balcombe Viaduct on the main line to Brighton, to Uckfield and then on to Hailsham. Earthworks were well advanced to the north-east of Haywards Heath, in all for about 1.25 miles to the north of Lingfield, and construction had also commenced in the vicinity of Uckfield extending to about 0.75 miles from the proposed junction south-west of Uckfield on the recently opened Tunbridge Wells to Lewes line. It is still possible to see part of the route of this abandoned line on Google Earth, marked by lines of trees. A continuation of the Ouse Valley line had been authorised from Hailsham to St Leonards, and this was abandoned prior to construction being commenced. A third recently authorised line which was abandoned was the Surrey and Sussex Junction which would have run from Croydon to Tunbridge Wells via Oxted. A contractor had been appointed and work was proceeding, including the boring of the long tunnel under the North Downs between Oxted and Woldingham, and the shorter tunnel at Cowden. The incomplete works show clearly on the Ordnance Survey 6 inch maps of the area for 1868-9. In this case, the scheme was eventually completed in 1884 to East Grinstead (in part as a joint line with the SER) and 1888 to Ashurst Junction.

In West Sussex, three lines were abandoned. The Chichester and Midhurst had been authorised in 1864, and construction was in hand in various sections near Cocking and Singleton. Contemporary Ordnance Survey maps show that the tunnel south of Singleton had been opened out, and the line is marked in outline around Cocking. Construction appears to have petered out south of Singleton. The works were abandoned in 1868, the incomplete line remaining untouched until a contractor was engaged in 1879, and it was eventually opened in 1881.

An extension of this railway north of Midhurst to connect with the LSW north of Petersfield was authorised in 1865, but no construction ever took place on this line, which would have resulted in Midhurst having lines to it from four directions.

**Railway construction of the 19th century, but to be strictly accurate we should say it is the building of the Meon Valley line in the first years of the 20th. The operation seen here, tipping spoil to form an embankment, would have been identical in the building of all the lines mentioned in the text. Mechanical aids in the form of a 'steam navvy' (steam shovel) only came into being in the late 19th century and then worked hand in hand with muscle power both human and equine.**
*David Foster-Smith*

The convoluted arrangement at Dorchester (LSWR/SR/BR) which lasted beyond the end of steam until 1970. Seen here is the dead-end 'up' platform, access to which for trains from Weymouth was by running forward beyond the signal box and then reversing into the platform. The opposite 'down' platform was on the right hand side – partly visible with the rest hidden behind the bushes. This curious arrangement was a legacy of the attempt by the Southampton & Dorchester to push west towards Exeter by means of a more coastal route compared with the inland line from Salisbury via Yeovil. Even post-1970 it would be another sixteen years before passengers were saved the trek across what was then waste ground from the now isolated station building and facilities to the replacement 'up' platform.

The final line to be abandoned took some time for me to track down. The obscure West Sussex Junction Railway was authorised in 1864. It was nominally independent, but effectively under the control of the LBSC, and would have run eastwards from Hardham (on the Mid-Sussex line south of Pulborough) through Storrington to join the line from Christ's Hospital to Shoreham at Steyning. In 1865, a deviation at the western end of the line was authorised so that the line would have left the Mid-Sussex at Pulborough.

The abandoned lines in West Sussex would all have run through sparsely populated rural areas with limited traffic potential. The one line here that was built between Chichester and Midhurst could hardly be considered an unqualified success. For most of the year, a sparse service trundled along between the two towns. Singleton served nearby Goodwood, and for the annual race week, special services arrived from further afield including royal trains from London. It was hardly a recipe for prosperity, and the line lost its passenger service in 1935, the weekly goods following in 1951 (apart from a stub to Lavant) when the unfortunate C2x class 0-6-0 No32522 plunged into a collapsed culvert south of Midhurst.

Several of the abandoned lines (including the London, Lewes & Brighton) were located in a narrow corridor in East Surrey and East Sussex, where the competition for traffic between the LBSC, LCDR and SER was at a climax when the crash occurred. Without the banking collapse, the railway map of East Sussex would have developed rather differently.

As a result of the crisis, talks were also instituted with the SER over terms for a possible amalgamation of the two companies. In the event, the proposals came to nothing, but in 1869 an agreement with the SER was reached over pooling of receipts for traffic to and from Hastings which finished off any prospect of the construction of the Ouse Valley and St Leonards railways. (There were several amalgamation proposals over the years between the LBSC and the SER which all fizzled out.)

# The recession and economic recovery

The recession in railway construction continued until the end of the 1870s, but in the middle of this period there was one exceptional year (1874) when eight separate projects totalling eighty-seven route miles were opened, four by the LSWR, two by the LCDR, and one each by the SER and the Somerset & Dorset (S&D). The last of these was in many ways the most interesting as it involved the line over the Mendips, twenty-two miles of fearsome gradients, numerous tunnels and viaducts in a desperate attempt by the S&D to establish a link to Bristol and the Midlands. Whilst it succeeded in this aim, linking up with the Midland Railway at Bath, the financial drain on the railway's resources was severe and drove it to the brink of bankruptcy.

The S&D made overtures to the GWR, which was on the verge of taking over its affairs, when the GWR advised the LSWR of the proposals under the terms of an agreement that the two companies had, and not for the first time the LSWR outmanoeuvred the GWR, this time in partnership with the Midland Railway. Over the course of a few days the S&D were presented with an offer that they could not refuse and so in 1875 came into being the Somerset and Dorset Joint Railway by means of a hastily drawn up lease on terms favourable to the S&D.

I am unsure why there was such a proliferation of schemes in 1874; maybe economic conditions ameliorated during the immediately preceding years to encourage investment, or maybe it was just coincidence. Perhaps you might have some ideas. Whatever the cause, 1874 proved to be something of a false dawn for those looking for economic recovery as in the following years construction rates fell back to the levels of the early 1870s. Not until 1880 and after did the amount of construction rise, but by this time the opportunities to extend the network had significantly reduced (except perhaps in the West Country).

The LBSC eventually recovered financial stability by the late 1870s after a lengthy period of retrenchment and economising. Some of the schemes authorised prior to the banking collapse were built and opened: Horsham to Leatherhead opened in 1867; Hayling Island (1867); Groombridge, Uckfield and Lewes (1868); Peckham Rye to Sutton (1868); lines to Wimbledon from Streatham (1868: joint with LSWR); the Central Croydon branch (1868 and definitely to prove to be a white elephant); and the Kemp Town branch (1869). Apart from some minor construction, no further new lines were opened by the LBSC from 1869 until 1880.

After 1880, in addition to the Oxted lines delayed by the banking crisis (this partly completed as a joint line with the SER), the LBSC opened the Cuckoo Line from Hailsham to Redgate Mill Junction (1880); Chichester to Midhurst (also abandoned earlier in the banking crisis) (1881); the Bluebell Line from East Grinstead to Culver Junction (1882); and the Devil's Dyke branch (1887). Its most significant construction during this time was also the last line to open, the Quarry Line from Coulsdon to Earlswood, providing a fast, independent route between London and Brighton avoiding the congestion at Redhill which Parliament's strange decision back in the 1830s had given rise to. The line opened for freight in 1899 and for passenger use in 1900 (perhaps, in strict terms, a widening of the main line, albeit with an independent route).

The SER also more or less ceased new construction until the end of the 1870s, the only new line being Sandling Junction to Sandgate, opened in 1874. There followed a late flowering of railway construction in Kent, with the SER opening lines between Greenwich and Charlton (1878); Grove Park to Bromley North (1878); Westerham branch (1881); Elmers End to Hayes (1882); Hundred of Hoo (1882); New Romney and Dungeness (1883-4); Canterbury to Cheriton (1887); Hawkhurst (1892-3); Dartford Loop (1895); Purley to Tadworth

**James Staats Forbes 1823-1904.** Forbes was a draftsman in the office of Brunel and eventually rose to the position of Goods Manager with the GWR. Later he was reputedly offered the position of General Manager of that company but instead took over the failing LCDR as GM and was subsequently appointed chairman in 1873. In addition to this he held several other senior board positions with other concerns as well as at various times with three other railway companies the Hull & Barnsley, Whitechapel & Bow, and Didcot, Newbury & Southampton.

(1897) and on to Tattenham Corner (1901); and Crowhurst to Bexhill West (1902), the last two coming into being after the working agreement with the LCDR had been concluded.

The LCDR responded with Maidstone to Ashford (1884); Fawkham to Gravesend Pier (1886); and Shortlands to Nunhead (1892).

By the time of the creation of the working committee in 1899 (the South Eastern and Chatham Railway was not a formal merger of the two companies, both of which remained in existence until the 1923 grouping), virtually every significant town in Kent had railway services operated by both the SER and the LCDR. The only town which the LCDR had not reached was Folkestone which was included in a pooling agreement. The SER had representation in every town of any size in Kent.

On the Isle of Wight, there were some interesting schemes promoted at about the time of the crash, none more so than the unfortunate Isle of Wight (Newport Junction), promoted in 1867 which struggled to build a line from Sandown to Newport, finally achieving this in 1879 having reached Shide about a mile to the south in 1875. Also opening in 1875 was the Ryde and Newport which together with the C&N and the IW (NJ) eventually merged to form the impecunious Isle of Wight Central Railway.

These lines were joined by the Brading Harbour line of the IWR in 1882, the Freshwater, Yarmouth and Newport in 1889 (remaining independent until 1923), and the Ventnor West branch (1897-1900) which was absorbed into the IWC. The only involvement of the mainland companies was the line from Ryde Pier Head to St Johns Road, opened in 1880 after a decade of frustration when passengers had to travel through Ryde by horse drawn tram. This line was jointly owned by the LSWR and LBSC, but operated entirely by the IWC & IWR.

The LSWR was least affected by the crisis, and continued to open new lines throughout the 1870s, particularly in the West Country where it reached Torrington (1872); Lydford (with access via the GWR to Plymouth) and Sidmouth and

**One of the tunnels on the Chichester to Midhurst railway, one of many lines, not just in the south, which never aspired to the anticipatory heights of the promoters. Opened in 1881 it retained a passenger service until only 1935 thereafter seeing freight workings as late as 1991 from Lavant south to Chichester.**

Ilfracombe in 1874; and to Holsworthy (1879). In the London area, it opened to Gunnersbury in 1869 (and thereby secured an important link through West London for freight); the line through Aldershot from Pirbright to Farnham Junction (1870); then to the west of Southampton, Bournemouth Central from Christchurch (1870); Broadstone to Poole (1872) and to Bournemouth West (1874). The line to Portsmouth Harbour followed (joint with LBSC, 1878); and Ascot to Frimley (1878).

On into the 1880s and '90s and the LSWR continued to consolidate its network, opening suburban lines in the London area such as Surbiton to Guildford via Cobham; and Effingham Junction to Leatherhead (1885); Putney to Wimbledon, better known today as part of the District Line (1889); and filling in the missing sections of the direct line to Bournemouth and beyond (1885, 1888 and 1893). It was particularly active in Devon and North Cornwall, finally connecting with the Bodmin and Wadebridge in 1895 with a line from Meldon Junction, and then on to Padstow (1899); it reached Bude in 1898. It also completed a number of minor and branch lines, for instance the Swanage branch (1885) and Netley to Fareham (1889), some designed to keep out the GWR, such as Hurstbourne to Fullerton Junction (1885). In 1890, it secured an independent main line to Plymouth thanks to the Plymouth, Devonport and South Western line south from Lydford. In 1898, the Lynton and Barnstaple opened, the only passenger carrying narrow gauge line to come into the Southern Railway. In complete contrast, 1898 also saw the opening of the Waterloo and City line, the LSWR's only deep tube line.

By the commencement of the twentieth century, the network was almost complete, but a few late stragglers were added including the Basingstoke and Alton (1901); Axminster to Lyme Regis (1903); the Meon Valley line (1903); the line from Amesbury to Bulford (1906). The last line to open before the dark days of WW1 was, perhaps surprisingly, the independent PDSW branch to Callington (1908).

The Southern Railway added seven lines after the grouping, one to sort out the messy arrangements in Thanet, two to accommodate the growing suburbs of south-west London, two to nascent holiday resorts and two primarily freight lines. The Fawley branch (1925) served the developing oil industry to the west of Southampton Water, and the North Devon and Cornwall (1925) replaced a narrow gauge line serving clay extraction south of Torrington. In both cases passenger traffic was something of an afterthought. In 1926, a new connection between the SER and LCDR lines in Thanet was opened, including a new station at Dumpton Park, with redundant lines and stations closed at Margate (SER) and Ramsgate (LCDR). Then in 1929-30 the line from Wimbledon to Sutton opened, serving the vast new LCC estate at St Helier; this was followed by the Allhallows branch in 1932 (the holiday resort was unfortunately a complete failure); a realignment of the New Romney branch in 1937 with new stations at Lydd-on-Sea and Greatstone-on-Sea; and finally the Chessington branch opened in 1938-39, the intention of pushing on to Leatherhead frustrated by the war and post-war green belt policy.

Of all the lines not to have been built in the south, the Ouse Valley Railway is surely the one that is most lamented. Intended to link Haywards Heath, Uckfield and Hailsham, work on this 20-mile line started in May 1866 but was suspended in February 1867 never to resume. Even so in those few months much had been achieved and R. C. Riley recorded several views along the incompleted course on a visit in August 1950. Seen here are earthworks near Uckfield and an almost completed bridge nearby.
*The Transport Treasury*

## Conclusions

When I started out on this research project, I had no idea whether or not it would produce any meaningful results. I knew a little about the development of the Victorian railway network and some general background about the Railway Mania, and the collapse of Overend Gurney in 1866. Logic suggested that these events ought to be mirrored in the rates of railway construction, and I think the raw data and the bar charts bear this out. The peak caused by the Railway Mania is particularly marked, followed by the boom of the early 1860s when money was easy to come by. Of course, by 1866, much of the network had been completed and the pace of new construction would have tailed off even if the banking crisis had not occurred, but the abrupt fall in new construction once committed schemes had been completed by about 1868 is particularly noticeable. I found the stories of abandoned schemes in East Surrey and Sussex particularly fascinating, with every possibility that Brighton might have secured a second main line to London, perhaps with LCDR and SER express trains headed up by the locomotives of Martley, Kirtley, Stirling and Wainwright; and the abandoned Ouse Valley line, projected mainly to block competition for Eastbourne traffic and likely to prove to be a white elephant as it headed across the rural East Sussex Weald.

Today, few will be aware of Overend, Gurney and Company, and the devastating effect its failure had on the Victorian economy. Quite how these things are measured is not something I entirely understand, but in economic terms, it was the worst market failure until the 1929 Wall Street collapse, and that has since been eclipsed by the most recent 2008 banking collapse. There are a great many parallels between the events of 1866 and those of 2008. The Victorian economy was strongly based on industrialisation and engineering, so it is not surprising that railways were particularly affected after the crash. Measuring its effects in terms of railway construction is just one way of judging the impact; I imagine that locomotive and rolling stock construction also took quite a hit, and that passenger and freight receipts (and therefore profit and loss accounts) would also have been affected, but I am not tempted to try to research either. The other major railway company to fail during this time was the North British in faraway Scotland.

## References

'The Illustrated History of Railways in Britain', by Geoffrey Freeman Allen, published by Marshall Cavendish, 1979. A good general background to the history of railway development in Britain, particularly useful for information on the Railway Mania.

'The Railway Surveyors', by Gordon Biddle, published by Ian Allan, 1990. A full history of the role of the surveyor in the development and management of the railways, 1800-1990.

'Railway Archive' Nos 32, 33 & 34 'The History of the London, Chatham and Dover Railway' by G.A. Sekon, published by Lightmoor Press. Reprint of 1919/20 articles in 'Railway & Travel Monthly'. No 33 contains a good account of the impact of the Overend Gurney collapse, and the relationship between the LCDR and its contractor.

'Samuel Morton Peto – A Victorian Entrepreneur' by Adrian Vaughan, published by Ian Allan, 2009. A full biography of the contractor including his work for the LCDR and the 1866 banking collapse.

https://www.bankofengland.co.uk/-/media/boe/files/quarterly-bulletin/2016/the-demise-of-overend-gurney. Paper entitled 'The demise of Overend Gurney' by Rhiannon Sowerbutts. A surprisingly readable paper outlining the issues which gave rise to the 1866 banking crisis.

'Atlas of the Southern Railway', by Richard Harman and Gerry Nichols, published by Ian Allan. Comprehensive track diagrams and route mileage information for all Southern Railway lines.

'The London & South Western Railway', by O.S. Nock, published by Ian Allan, 1971

'The South Eastern and Chatham Railway', by O.S. Nock, published by Ian Allan, 1971

'The London Brighton and South Coast Railway', by C. Hamilton Ellis, published by Ian Allan, 1971. These three provided much of the information required to establish opening dates. Long out of print, more recent sources were also consulted.

'Points and Signals', by Michael Robbins, published by George Allen and Unwin, is a compilation of essays and includes one on the Ouse Valley Railway, and another on the IW(NJ). Both are reprints from 'The Railway Magazine' Nos 97 (1951) and 105 (1959), now both available on line at http://www.semgonline.com/RlyMag/OuseValleyRly.pdf and http://www.semgonline.com/RlyMag/IoWNewportJuncRailway.pdf

'Abandoned Railways of the LBSCR', G.A. Sekon, The Railway Magazine, Nov and Dec 1947, now available on line at http://www.semgonline.com/RlyMag/AbandonedLinesLBSCR.pdf

http://www.railwaytrains.co.uk/ouse1.html and http://www.railwaytrains.co.uk/ouse2.html This website explores the history of the Ouse Valley Railway, and includes a number of photographs of the remains of this abandoned railway.

'An Illustrated History of the Lewes and East Grinstead Railway', by Klaus Marx, published by the Oxford Publishing Company, 2000, contains details of the failed Beckenham, Lewes and Brighton Railway of 1863 and the abandoned London, Lewes and Brighton scheme of 1866.

'The Railways of Beckenham', by Andrew Hajducki, published by the Ardgour Press in association with Noodle Books, 2011, also includes a brief account of the abandoned London, Lewes and Brighton scheme of 1866.

# A 'Britannia' at Portsmouth and North Camp
## Images by Paul Cooper

**No 70000** *Britannia* **paused at the photo stop at North Camp on the outward journey. From this perspective one might be excused for thinking only a few of the participants had bothered to alight to record the scene, but...** *Paul Cooper collection*

On 4 October 1964 the Locomotive Club of Great Britain organised the 'Vectis Railtour' operating from London to Portsmouth and thence by ferry to the Isle of Wight and a journey over most of the surviving Island rail network.

At Waterloo a nine coach train had been assembled comprising SR set No 237 plus buffet car and in the order of BSK, 4xSO, RKB, 2xSO and a final BSK. In charge from Waterloo as far as Guildford, via Clapham Junction, Twickenham, Staines Central, Ascot, Camberley, Ash Vale, Aldershot and Ash was 'Q1' No 33026. Departure was half a minute early at 9.04½ although time was then lost all the way to Guildford so that by the time Guildford was reached the special was already 25 late. No reason was given for the delays.

*Above:* ...from a slightly different perspective it appears most of the train had in fact disembarked. The streaks on the boiler casing appear to be bird-droppings.
*Roger Thornton*

*Left:* **A Nine Elms crew worked the train on the mainland. The driver (hanging out of the cab) is Bill Plumb and the fireman Alan Newman.**
*Paul Cooper collection*

## A 'Britannia' at Portsmouth and North Camp

Notwithstanding an engine change where No 70000 came on the other end, a six minute saving was achieved and the tour continued via Ash, North Camp (photo stop of seven minutes), Wokingham, Reading General, Basingstoke, Winchester City, Eastleigh, Botley and Fareham to Portsmouth Harbour. The original schedule had been for a 13.50 arrival ready for the 14.35 sailing to Ryde and no doubt there were a few concerned travellers wondering if they might even miss the sailing scheduled for 14.35. As it was, the same 25 minute late running continued, No. 70000 and crew unable to better the time, so resulting in a 14.10 arrival at the Harbour station, but still with 25 minutes to alight and embark.

At Ryde Pier Head a six-coach train was waiting – no restaurant car this time (were there ever such luxuries on Island trains….?) – and 'O2' No 14 was used for a return run to Ventnor. Back again at Pier Head No 14 was detached and sister engine No 28 came on the country end, this time taking the train to Newport where unfortunately a derailment between Newport and Cowes precluded the intended destination of Cowes being reached. Consequently it was a run-round at Newport and return once more to Ryde ready for the 18.30. The saving in time resulting from the slightly curtailed route also assisted as the return to Ryde was at 18.18½, ready for the 18.30 sailing.

Back at Portsmouth, No 70000 was again in charge and left one minute early at 19.16. There was then a relatively easy return run along the 'Portsmouth Direct' where arrival at Waterloo was again late, delayed this time by five minutes to 20.52.

**Portsmouth Harbour – and still those safety valves are lifted. Note too that No 70000 has lost its smoke-deflector handrails, replaced by handholds. At the time the engine was allocated to '5A', Crewe North.** *Paul Cooper collection*

# Pat Harmer, Polegate Signalman
## Interviewed by David Vaughan

Patrick Harmer, hereafter referred to as Pat, was born in May 1933 at Brightling in East Sussex and near the Obelisk known as 'Brightling Needle', one of 'Mad Jack' Fuller's follies.[1] In 1937 Pat's family moved to Battle Road in Hailsham which was to be his home until his marriage to his beloved wife Mabel in 1954. Hailsham was a busy market town and was effectively on the front line of wartime Britain, especially during the period known as 'The Battle of Britain'. Pat has memories of wartime bombings and airborne combat overhead and his attendance at the local secondary school was often interrupted by trips to the air raid shelters.

Pat Harmer in his first job as a junior porter at Polegate station.

## Pat Harmer, Polegate Signalman

Pat left school in 1948 and went out into the world of work. He told me that, 'In 1948 jobs were fairly easy to come by and I decided to join the railway, having been assured by my elders and betters that it could be a job for life, with opportunity for promotion and a pension at the end.' So it was that on 25 July, at 9.00am prompt, Pat attended a job interview with a Mr Earnshaw who was the station master at Polegate station. Pat added, 'It was obvious to me that this gentleman was what I would later refer to in my career as "One of the old school".'

Shortly afterwards Pat remembers attending a medical examination at Brighton works and, never having been anywhere near a place of such industrial size and activity, he was impressed by the assembly lines which, at that time, were engaged on building the three classes of Bulleid Pacifics. He was passed fit and commenced his employment as a junior Porter at Polegate station.

PH: The railways had only just been nationalised but I was in fact still starting work in a Southern Railway environment with many locomotives and much of the rolling stock still bearing Southern Railway logos.

DV: What did your duties as a junior porter entail?

PH: I was tasked with the general cleaning of the station area, checking passenger's tickets and dealing with excess fares. My first wages were £2.10 shillings a week with an extra payment for Sunday working. The job provided a good grounding for my future years on the railway. The discipline was strict but, provided you did your job properly there were no real problems. After about six months I was appointed to the permanent staff and so had my foot on the first rung of a railway career.

DV: Polegate must have been a busy station then with all the trains for Hastings and Eastbourne as well as the Cuckoo line trains to Tunbridge Wells and the freight traffic?

PH: Yes it was: in 1948 there were probably about 100 railway employees of one department or another working at, or attached to, Polegate. Mind you, by the time I retired in 1998, what with the closure of the Tunbridge Wells branch and the decline in freight traffic, the number of employees at the station had fallen to just six.

DV: How long did you remain at Polegate?

PH: Well, initially it was only for three years because in 1951 I was called up for National Service. In the meantime my dad, who had been a bricklayer, also went to work on the railways as a platelayer, stationed at Berwick just up the line.

DV: So how was army life?

PH: After basic training at various bases in Britain I was attached to the 49th Field Regiment of the Royal Artillery on 25 pounder field guns. We were based at Shorncliffe camp near Folkestone whilst fortunately my railway concessionary travel pass meant that I could get home on leave quite easily – that is, until we were posted to Cyprus for a spell of duty there. I was demobbed in August 1953.

DV: Did you return to your railway job straight away?

PH: Yes. I attended an interview, this time with the Divisional Superintendent at Redhill. He asked what I would like to choose as a career move and, when I said I would like to be a signalman, I was offered three jobs there and then, however all would have meant staying in lodgings. I felt that, after two years away from home I could not accept any of these posts, so I returned to Polegate as a relief porter until a vacancy for a signalman arose nearer my home.

DV: What can you tell me about your time as a relief porter?

PH: Well, on the whole, it was very interesting. Some of the work involved being at various goods depots in the district; and I also attended a shunting school course at Norwood and passed out successfully as both a goods and passenger shunter. Part of my duties as a relief porter was also as cover for sickness and annual leave on various level crossings that were normally covered by a resident crossing-keeper. On the main Brighton to Hastings line I worked at Milton Street, between Polegate and Berwick, and Selmeston, between Berwick and Glynde. These were usually on a twelve hour shift

**Polegate station looking east towards Eastbourne and Hastings. The train seen approaching from the direction of Lewes is the 'Sunny South Express' having come south from Liverpool, Sheffield and Manchester (presumably different portions?) and thence to Birmingham, Willesden and Kensington where the SR would take over responsibility. Likely at different times, differing origins and destinations applied but so far as the SR was concerned the train seen here (hauled by 'U1' Mogul No 31897) would likely split at Polegate with separate portions for Eastbourne and Hastings. Elsewhere on the Southern, a portion of the same train also served Herne Bay, Margate and Ramsgate.**

basis, the hours being 0600-1800hrs and 1800-0600hrs. You have to bear in mind that, in the mid-1950s, there was not so much road traffic to contend with and, as a result, some of these jobs were in fact rather boring at times. At other times I covered crossings on the 'Cuckoo line' between Polegate and Hailsham. These were at Otham Court (No73 gate), Sayerlands (No74 gate) and at Mulbrooks where the B2104 road from Hailsham to Stone Cross crossed the line. Although these jobs were interesting in their own way they were quite relaxed by comparison to some of my other duties, especially at night-time, when it was exceptionally quiet and you could feel as one with nature, only the foxes, badgers and owls as company.

PH: Another of my duties whilst based at Polegate was as a signal lampman. For this duty you had to be fit and certainly not frightened of heights as some of the signal posts were nearly 50 feet high. The weather was also an issue; in summer when the sun was shining and the birds were singing, it was all very nice but in the winter in the snow, rain and wind it was a very different story. I remember that there was a shunt signal between the tracks and while I was changing the lamps it came on to rain so I went to the mess room and grabbed a long mac. As I crossed over the tracks to the shunt signal I felt a jolt like a rabbit punch in the back of my neck. I realised that there must have been a moment as I crossed the third rail that the current had jumped across – I got out of the road fast. Because of its weight, the mac had a short brass chain to hang it up with and, when I got back and took it off I felt my neck and the chain had burnt its impression in my skin so I certainly had had a lucky escape. If I remember rightly there were about fifty different lamps at Polegate on the various signals operated by the three signal boxes in the area. These signal lamps required cleaning and filling with paraffin twice a week. This work was done on a rotating basis and was carried out on the early shift, which was 5.15am -1.40pm, during which time three hours would be taken up with lamping duties.

DV: So when did your life as an actual signalman begin?

PH: Well in 1954 I married my wife Mabel and we moved into a rented house in Eastbourne. I undertook training as a signalman at Norwood and Seaford and I qualified as a signalman in March 1956. Soon afterwards a vacancy came up for a signalman's position in Seaford, which I successfully applied for. My duties at Seaford involved both signal box and platform work and again looking after the lamps which I was used to. The signal box was situated at the end of the platform and with the station not very far from the sea, it could be rather a windy post at times. The box consisted of a twenty-four lever frame with Tyers block instruments. Although passenger trains were mainly electric multiple units in 1956, there was still a fair amount of steam worked freights. As Seaford was a terminus station there was also a fair amount of run-round and shunting moves, hence it was a good place to learn the signalman's trade.

*Below and opposite:* Berwick signal box, interior and exterior. The box here dates from 1879. The interior view depicts equipment from a mixture of eras. SR 3-position block instrument and associated tapper bell, and basically what were simply distant, home and starting signals for both up and down lines. The short levers indicate either colour light operation or motor-operated mechanical signals.

37

DV: How long were you at Seaford?

PH: I suppose it was about a year and then I was promoted to the box at Stone Cross Junction. This was on the line that ran directly from Polegate to Pevensey (the now lifted top section of the Polegate/Eastbourne triangle which meant that trains could run straight through to Hastings and beyond without reversing at Eastbourne). This was known in local railway circles as 'over the top'. The signal box at Stone Cross had a seventeen lever frame and again with Tyers block instruments. Access to the box was by way of the road bridge at Friday Street a quarter of a mile away via the track so you had to be very safety conscious when walking the route. I remember one morning I was walking the track from the bridge to the box with a mate and it was thick fog. We were talking and not really paying as much attention as we should have been, when all of a sudden out of the fog we saw the light of an electric unit with the 18 headcode. It was too close for comfort so we both leaped out of the way. It would have been doubtful if the driver saw us and, in any case he would never have been able to stop.

PH: Stone Cross box was very isolated and all we had for company was the local wildlife of which, in those days, there was quite a variety. There was no running water or flush toilet facilities so water and other supplies were delivered by train. The chap who I took over the box from told me that there used to be a permanent way inspector, no longer living, whose mother lived at Stone Cross and he used to walk the track from there back home to Hampden Park. He told me that sometimes on a quiet night you could allegedly hear his footsteps passing the box. Well, I thought it a good tale, but one night I did in fact hear footsteps on the track. I looked out but could not see anyone there. There was of course probably a perfectly rational explanation for this but, you never know. Part of the signalman's job at Stone Cross, apart from looking after our own signal lamps, was to look after those on the line north of Hampden Park so once again we had to walk along the lineside and keep a sharp eye open for trains in all weathers. We carried a lamp of course but there was no high-vis clothing in those days.

*Below and opposite:* **Hampden Park signal box inside and out. This box opened in 1888 with the frame progressively extended from 14, then 17 and finally to 24 levers in 1930. The final change necessitated the none too attractive extension to the main structure – note at the time of the photograph a reduction to 20 levers had occurred and with the levers in use, restricted to running line signals and just a single crossover. Again 3-position block instruments and also 21st century computer equipment.**

## Pat Harmer, Polegate Signalman

DV: You went on to work at Polegate for some time didn't you?

PH: Yes. In 1958 a position for a signalman at Polegate 'B' box, otherwise known as East Junction, became vacant. I applied and was duly appointed. This was the post I had been waiting for and it was where I really learnt my job, as in 1958 it was a really busy box. You name it and we worked it. Track circuits had started to come in which also made things a bit easier. The box consisted of a sixty-one lever frame controlled by standard SR three position block instruments, a much more reliable method than I had previously used.

DV: What sort of traffic did the box handle over a typical shift?

PH: This was mainly passenger, with services to Brighton, Hastings, London, and of course the Tunbridge Wells branch, better known to locals as 'The Cuckoo line'. In 1958 there was also still a fair amount of freight traffic. Most passenger trains were EMUs but there was some steam on both passenger and nearly all the goods trains. The steam locomotives consisted of Bulleid Light Pacifics, 'Schools', Q1s, Moguls and Standard tanks. On Summer Saturdays we had inter-regional services to and from Wolverhampton, Manchester and Sheffield bound for Eastbourne and Hastings.

On return journeys it was often the case that a portion from both these destinations would join up at Polegate. With all the subsequent locomotive movements, light engine and filling-in turns, etc., Saturdays were pretty busy. There were times when I relieved a colleague at Polegate B on a Saturday at 1.00pm and literally took over the lever frame as he stepped off it.

DV: Polegate had quite an extensive system of sidings for goods as I recall?

PH: Yes, there were four freight yards at Polegate. They were the up-side yard, which consisted of about eight sidings with access to the main line via the London end of the station or via the Polegate level crossing box. This location today is where there is a housing estate known as Heron Ridge. I don't know about herons but I've seen plenty of magpies there! The old yard was situated on the down side where the present Co-op car park is located. This yard consisted of about five sidings mostly dealing with coal and brick traffic with access to the High Street. We also had a cattle dock, which was located between the old yard and the station. The entrance and exit to all of these yards was controlled by the signalman at Polegate A box, or the West Box as it was also known. The two other yards were known as the East and West section and were situated adjacent to the down Hastings line, the part of the triangle we referred to as being 'over the top'. In two of the sidings in the West section it was possible to stable as many as 365 wagons – I always remember as it was the same as the number of days in a year.

Bardick hand lamp, plastic cased signal repeaters and plastic release plungers have replaced the old paraffin lamp, brass cased repeaters, and similar brass release plungers – the transitional phase between the old and what would eventually sweep away structures such as this to be combined into what are now referred to as 'control centres'.

DV: I think I remember these sidings, didn't they used to use them to break up the old wooden wagons?

PH: That's right, in the early 1960s the up-side became the break-up yard for all the freight wagons which had become surplus to requirements. These were unfitted wagons known in railway terms as 'highs', 'minerals' and 'lows'. They also broke up PMVs. This process was very labour intensive and could at times be dangerous; accidents were not infrequent in those days. They would set fire to the timber bodies but as the sidings had all been built up on loco waste, ash, etc., we used to see puffs of smoke coming up through the track. If you went out with a crowbar and poked it down into the ballast it came out quite hot. These fires under the track spread and got a bit close to the main line, so in the end when most of the sidings had been lifted, they had to get a digger in and cut a series of trenches and fill them with fullers' earth. The result was it eventually put the underground fires out and we had the advantage of lovely blackberries alongside the track the next autumn whilst the resident rabbits got centrally heated burrows!

DV: How long was your stay at Polegate?

PH: As I have said, Polegate B was a busy box and so I welcomed the chance to get some experience as a crossing keeper which I did for a spell in 1962 when I went to work at Wilmington level crossing situated about half way between Polegate and Berwick. As it happened I had chosen to change jobs just before the country experienced one of the worst winters for many years. It had started to snow hard during the night. About 3.00am I remember seeing the snow gradually starting to drift over the tracks and up the gates. At that crossing there was little road traffic so it was normal practice to keep the gates open for rail traffic but closed to the road. I heard the early morning paper train, about 6.00am on the Sunday morning, steam-hauled of course, leaving Berwick and listened out as it cleared its path through the drifts. Anyway it came through the

**Semi-modern day Eastbourne. A goods yard with limited, if any, traffic, and the modern railway operated by multiple units so removing the need for stock storage sidings and engine release crossovers.**

crossing all right and made it into Eastbourne but that was the last train that ran through for some time. They tried running six and even twelve car electrics through, with sparks from the shoes lighting the sky for miles around, but it was too frozen and they all got stuck. The snow lasted for many weeks, indeed the thaw did not really begin to set in until March 1963 and then, to cap it all, management decided to close Wilmington as a manual crossing and to change it to automatic half barriers. So, after only nine months I returned to my duties at Polegate B box.

DV: The 1960s saw a lot of changes on the railway all over the country and the Southern Region. The Beeching closures and the end of steam power being the most notable. How did these changes affect you?

PH: In the middle of the 60s the first diesels arrived in our neck of the woods. Initially these were the DEMUs which took over from steam on the Tunbridge Wells branch line and then there were the Crompton class 33s and the class 73 EDs. Both these classes were designed for mixed traffic working. In 1965 the Hailsham to Redgate Mill section of the Cuckoo Line was closed to passenger traffic although goods workings to and from Heathfield remained for a short time afterwards. Then in September 1968 the Polegate to Hailsham section closed and in January 1969 the direct route from Polegate to Stone Cross ('over the top') was taken out of use. As a result of these closures it was not long before only one signal box was required at Polegate.

DV: This must have affected your job, so what did you do next?

PH: Well, a vacancy arose for a relief signalman at Bexhill which I successfully applied for. I had to purchase some form of transport for me to travel between Polegate and Bexhill for the early morning starts and late finishes, so I bought a little Yamaha 50 motorcycle which served me well for four years. I did a lot of relief work at various signal boxes in the area and I was rarely out of work. The only problem was you could never tell where you would be from one week to the next, which was a bit hard on family life at the time. Then in 1975 a vacancy occurred for the position of rest day relief at my home station of Polegate and I ended up covering the same signal boxes but with a set roster so I could organise my life a bit better and make the most of my days off. The beauty of this job was that you were never in one place too long and so never got involved in local squabbles and, at this time, there seemed to be plenty of these.

PH: In 1987, after spending some fifteen years as a relief signalman I was promoted to a permanent job at Hampden Park signal box. Now 'The Park', as it was known to railwaymen, was a very busy box, no time to get bored there. The layout at Hampden Park was quite straight forward. The frame consisted of twenty-four levers, eleven of these being spares. The junction at Willingdon was over a quarter of a mile away and the points were electrically worked. All signalling was done by standard three position block. While I was resident at Hampden Park it was reported to be the busiest level crossing in England with the crossing closed to traffic for 35 minutes in every hour.

*Above and opposite:* **Eastbourne exterior. The MAS signal was not incorrectly displaying all three aspects simultaneously but instead it picked up the glare from a low sun. Inside we see part of the 72 lever rearward facing 1935 frame. Finally, Pat at work on the 1991 'NX' panel.**

DV: I believe you ended your railway career at Eastbourne; how did that come about?

PH: Yes, that's right. After three and a half years at Hampden Park my final promotional move was to Eastbourne in 1992. This was a totally different style of signalling comprising a solid state interlocking panel, SSI for short. Basically, instead of levers all movements were controlled by push buttons. This panel had been installed in April 1991 and had replaced a seventy-two lever frame which is, to this day, located in a different part of the box. To remove it would be a major undertaking so it remains as a sort of museum piece.

PH: I must admit to being apprehensive at first after so many years of working mechanical frames but, after working the new panel for a couple of weeks I even surprised myself and took to it like a duck to water. I have often reflected how much signalling operation had changed over my career. I am pleased to say that, even when the so-called state-of-the-art computer system arrived at Eastbourne, I managed to keep on top of it.

DV: Well, that takes us into the 90s. When did you actually retire from Eastbourne?

PH: My last shift was on 18 March 1998. They gave me a good send off and I have many memories of a long and eventful career with some good mates.

1. John Fuller (20 February 1757 – 11 April 1834), better known as "Mad Jack" Fuller (although he himself preferred to be called "Honest John" Fuller), was Squire of the hamlet of Brightling, in Sussex, and a politician who sat in the House of Commons between 1780 and 1812. He was a builder of follies, philanthropist, patron of the arts and sciences, and a supporter of slavery. He purchased and commissioned many paintings from J.M.W. Turner. He was sponsor and mentor to Michael Faraday.
See – https://en.wikipedia.org/wiki/Mad_Jack_Fulle

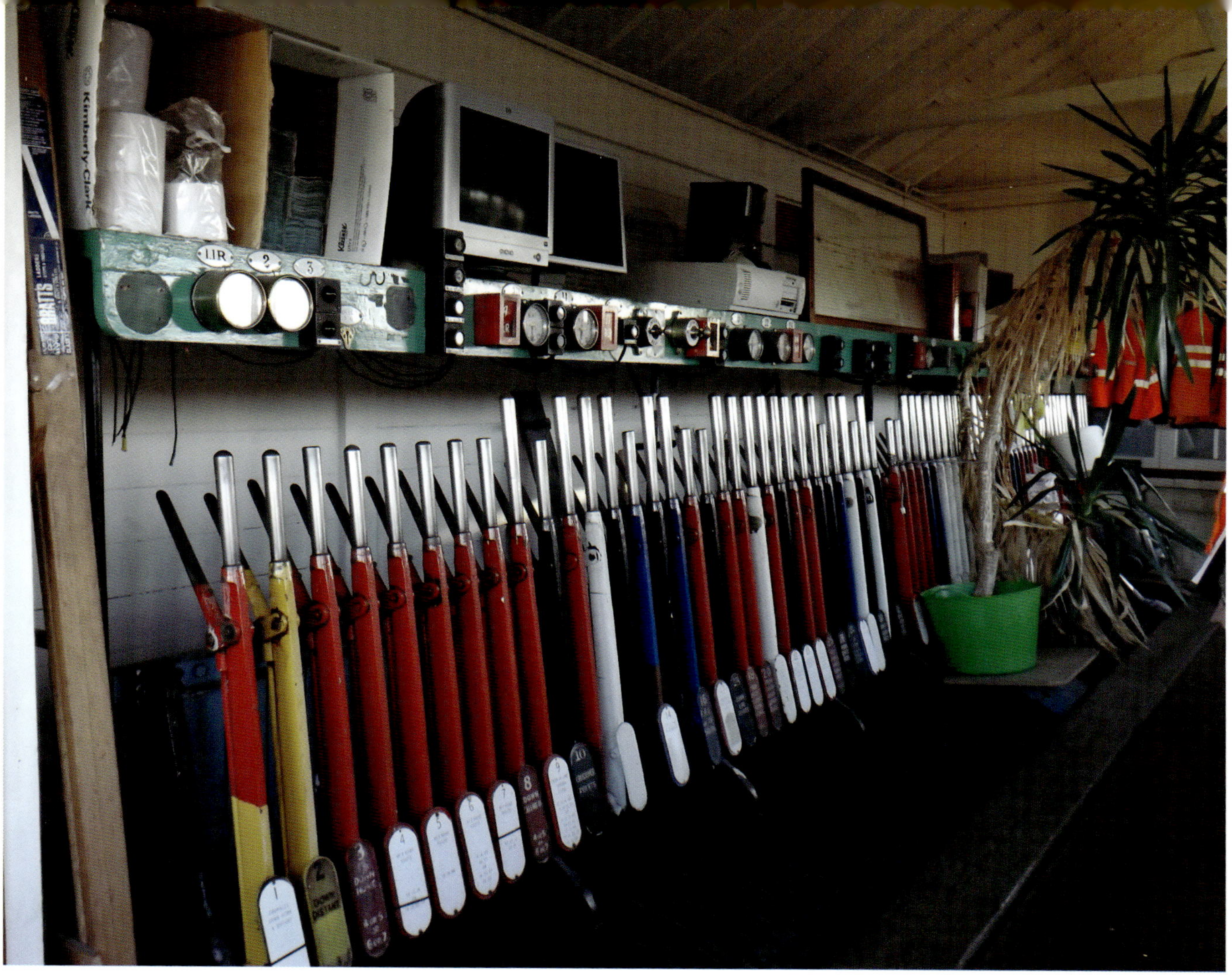
Kimberly-Clark
11R
2
3

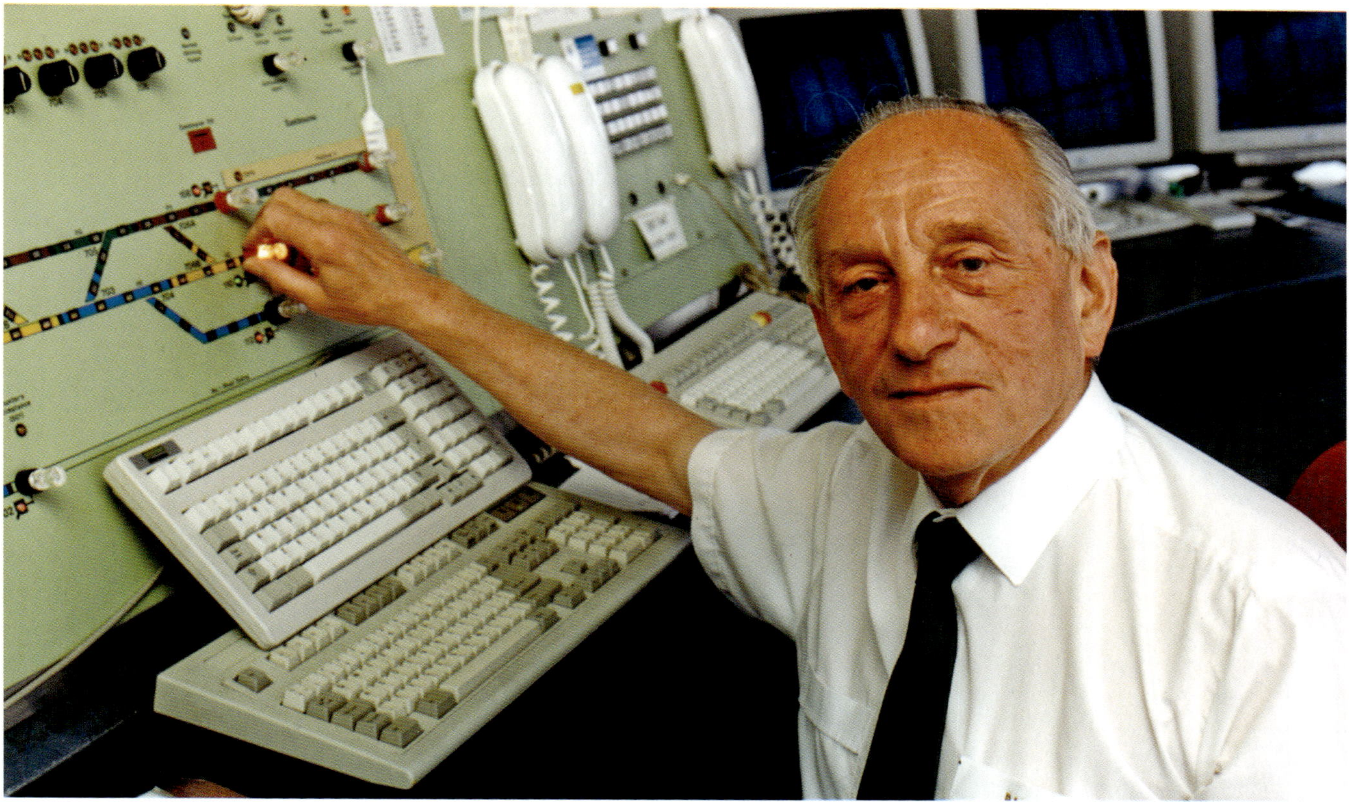

# (More) Southern Railway Inspections

## Compiled by Gerry Nichols

Memorandum of inspection in the West of England, 17, 18 and 19 August 1937.

Present:

| | |
|---|---|
| Mr R. Holland-Martin | Chairman * |
| Sir Herbert Walker | General Manager |
| Mr E. J. Missenden | Traffic Manager |
| Mr G. Ellson | Chief Engineer |
| Mr C. F. de Pury | Divisional Superintendent |
| Mr W. H. Shortt | Divisional Engineer |
| Mr W. J. Harrington | Gen Asst to Traffic Manager |

\* Present 17 and 18 August.

1. Chilmark (between Dinton and Tisbury). Negotiations are proceeding with the Air Ministry for the provision of siding facilities to the Chilmark Depot, and the proposed point of connection was visited. Plan No10/2265 K/R.9 was produced showing the layout, including off loading, sidings run-round road, crossover between up and down main lines and signal box. It was noted that the Air Ministry had generally approved the scheme, and the final acceptance of the detailed terms is now awaited.

2. Templecombe. The works in connection with the reconstruction of Templecombe station in accordance with Traffic and Continental Minute of 28 May 1936 were inspected. It was noted that the extension of the main line platforms has been completed.

3. Axminster. There is difficulty at present in transferring luggage from the Down platform to the Lyme Regis trains in the Up Bay. Consideration was given to Plan No10/2272 P/M.14 showing how an overhead gallery and lifts could be provided at an estimated cost of £2,240. It was thought, however, that a less costly scheme might be prepared with two inclined conveyors and an elevated roller path. The Chief Engineer will pursue the matter with the object of preparing a scheme as early as possible, to enable the facilities to be available for the summer traffic of next year.

As we have alluded to in previous issues, sometimes finding images to accompany a specific article can be difficult – if not impossible – and that has proved to be the case in attempting to find views of all the locations mentioned, let alone in the period in question. Consequently I hope readers will not mind too much if we include a short selection of West of England/Withered Arm views. Surely you cannot have too much of a good thing! We start with 'S15' No 30830 at the head of an up freight entering Sherborne on 31 July 1950. *P. A. Wells*

# (More) Southern Railway Inspections

**Next, another 'S15', this time No 30845 and on a down stopping train at Seaton Junction. No date although we do know it is the 2.08pm Axminster to Exeter Central service. It also begs the question, were the class fitted for steam-heat in winter?**

4. Seaton. The work in progress on the station remodelling was inspected. It was decided to provide a small elongated island within the Company's boundary on the station forecourt, with suitable 'in' and 'out' and parking direction notices. The Chief Engineer will arrange for a plan to be prepared. This arrangement will allow for better circulation of road traffic, and provide a definite standing space for the Associated Company's omnibuses. Plan No11/2623 D/5 shows a small triangular space marked as pavement outside the gates leading to the engine shed; it would be better if this were arranged as a bed and planted with suitable shrubs. The General Manager instructed the Chief Engineer to arrange accordingly.

5. Sidmouth Junction. The station was inspected and found to be in good condition. The General Manager decided that there is no justification for an extensive scheme of modernisation at present, but that the following items in the Committee's report might be carried out forthwith:

Provision of 'Tilley' lamps.

Station name plate on awning entrance over entrance from approach.

Indication signs and lamp signs.

(Second part) Artificial lighting in Ladies W.C.

The Chief Engineer will prepare an estimate for these items.

The Modernisation Report also included a proposal for fencing on the up, and down, platforms to enable the public to cross the trains when trains are obstructing the level crossing. As there are obvious objections to this, the Divisional Superintendent was instructed to consider the question of affording relief either by extending the up platform at the east end and/or moving the up starting signal outward, and report to the Traffic Manager.

6. Exmouth. Attention was called to the bad external condition of the plant of the cartage contractor Haynes. The Divisional Superintendent will follow up the matter.

7. Exeter Central.

(a) Warehouse Accommodation. The provision of additional warehouse accommodation is necessary to meet the many requests from traders, and the following plans were produced:

No10/2266.P/M.17. Addition of extra floor to existing Goods shed for storage purposes at a cost of £30,000. This would displace the existing Goods Office.

45

Next a classic Henry Casserley view. Adams 4-4-0 No 662 near Okehampton on 3 August 1928.

No10/2266.B/M.26. Utilisation of Queen Street frontage for a new Goods Office and Traders premises (Estimate £40,000).

The present Goods Shed is seventy-seven years old and has not a satisfactory layout from the working standpoint. It was decided that the suggested scheme was expensive and undesirable, and the General Manager instructed that plans should be prepared showing how a new Goods Shed could be erected with three storeys for warehousing, with direct road access to the first floor from Queen Street or from New North Road. It was arranged that a representative of the Superintendent of Operation should at once confer with the Divisional Superintendent and Divisional Engineer to enable an outline scheme to be prepared. In the meantime consideration to be given to the erection of a standard traders store at the foot of the bank adjacent to New North Road, in order to meet the immediate requirements. The Proposal to erect shops and offices on the Queen Street frontage Plan No10/2266•B/1426) to be dropped.

(b) Stabling accommodation for Passenger Stock. The Divisional Superintendent drew attention to the fact that it was necessary to stable passenger stock on the up and down through running roads at Exeter Central at peak periods. It was suggested that an additional carriage siding to hold seven or eight bogie vehicles should be positioned south of the existing siding No 5 adjacent to Messrs Rowes' garage. It was agreed that the Chief Engineer should submit a plan and estimate for this.

8. St. Budeaux – proposed widening of Wolseley Road. Plans showing the proposed road widening works of Plymouth City Council were considered. The scheme involves the acquisition by the Council of a strip of land now forming part of our goods yard. The first proposals of the Council, shown in pink on Plan No10/2270.K/L.13, would still leave sufficient room in the possession of the Company to allow for a rearrangement of the yard to provide an additional siding should it be found necessary. The latest proposals of the Council (indicated in pencil on the plan) involve the acquisition of a wider strip, and the rearrangement of the yard to provide an additional siding would result in a reduction of width of the cart road and would be unsatisfactory. It was decided that there was no objection to the first proposals by the Council, but that the Company should not agree to the latest scheme. It was noted that there is no need to enlarge the yard facilities at present, but the district is growing and it may be necessary in the future.

9. Ernesettle (Proposed siding for R.N.A.D. between Tamerton Foliot and St Budeaux). The R.N.A. depot was visited in company with Admiralty representatives. Plan No 10/2270/.K/L.16 shows the layout of the proposed siding in accordance with Admiralty requirements, the cost being estimated at £68,370. The work involved includes rock excavation and bridge widening, and it was suggested to the Admiralty engineers who were met on site that they might like to give consideration to a possible alternative and less costly scheme by moving the point of connection northward. This would probably obviate excavation and bridge widening, and construction could be carried out in a shorter time. It was arranged that the Chief Engineer should get in touch with the Superintending Civil Engineer at the Admiralty and discuss this alternative with him.

High above the town, No 34017 *Ilfracombe* crosses Tavistock viaduct with the 'ACE'. Again no exact date but circa 1955.

The same named train but in more serene surroundings. The single-coach portion of the named train arriving at Torrington behind 'M7' No 30034 on 6 September 1954. *A. F. Taylor*

**Shunting duty at Plymouth Friary, 2 September 1958. An 'O2' mingles with a 'Queen Mary' brake, gate-stock and the products of Mr Bulleid and BR.**
*L. W. Rowe*

10. Stonehouse Pool. The suggested provision of a new 3 tons Grafton crane authorised by Traffic & Continental minute 30 January 1936 was reviewed. The 1936 tonnage figure shows a decrease over 1935 owing to the reduction in trade of Messrs Sulfurophosphate. As it is anticipated that the traffic will pass again in the near future, the Divisional Superintendent was instructed to report further on the provision of the crane when the traffic handled justified this course.

11. Cattewater. A general inspection of the railway facilities at Cattewater was made; particular attention was called to the fact that Messrs National Fertilisers Ltd require certain alterations to be made to the Cattewater loading dock. The firm are now receiving large quantities of material inwards for blending purposes, but the facilities at present are not suitable for off-loading owing to the height of the dock. It was noted that the Divisional Superintendent is meeting Colonel Warrington of the firm on 23 August for a discussion as to the actual requirements, and possible terms, under which the accommodation might be provided.

12. Plymouth Friary (Improved Goods Office Accommodation). The offices were inspected, and plan No 10/2266.C/W8 was produced showing how the existing building could be improved at a cost of £500. The present office staff numbers seventeen.

Although it was agreed it was necessary to improve the accommodation, it was decided that the scheme shown on the plan is not wholly satisfactory, as two new lavatories would open directly from the general office and the staff would still be crowded. The Chief Engineer will therefore prepare a plan showing:

(a) The extension of the office building at the east end.

(b) The provision of two lavatories not opening directly from the General Office.

(c) The removal of Chaplin's cartage office (a timber structure) from the east end of the Goods Office to the opposite side of the shed approach road.

13. Plymouth North Road. Mr Pearson, Asst District Traffic Manager, and Mr Lake, Divisional Engineer (G.W.R.), were met informally at North Road, and they produced a plan showing in outline the scheme for the station reconstruction. The proposals include the replacement of the present structure by a station with additional and longer platforms, involving the widening of the bridge at the west end. As a part of the scheme it is proposed to close the entrance on the north side (except for mail traffic) and also to close Mutley Station. It was noted that certain preparatory work had commenced.

# Southampton Central to Redbridge

## Peter Tatlow

Near pristine No 30827, an 'S15' Class 4-6-0 built at Eastleigh in 1927, emerges from the tunnel and passes under the footbridge with the power station in the background on the morning of 3 July 1958 with a train of coaching stock. The position of the discs, however, causes some uncertainty. The BR Sectional Appendix for 1 October 1960 indicates 'light engine from west of Basingstoke to Eastleigh MPD', but this does not fit the bill. The Southern Railway Engine Head Signals booklet applicable from the beginning of 1944 gives two additional routes viz: Southampton Docks and Bournemouth West, via Sway and Romsey to Romsey, via Eastleigh and Redbridge. [35/9-20] *(All images are by the Author)*

The original London to Southampton Railway ran in to Southampton Terminus near the City centre, opening throughout on 11 May 1840, from where access was gained to the Old Docks. With the construction of the Southampton to Dorchester Railway westwards, the route out of the city was along the shores of Southampton Water until it reached Redbridge where it crossed the River Test. Due to delays in completing the tunnel to connect with the line from London, this opened from the west initially only to Blechynden on 1 June 1847, it only being completed to Southampton Junction on 29 July. This line was joined at Redbridge by one from Romsey on 6 March 1865.

When built, Blechynden station, renamed Southampton West in July 1858, was virtually on the water's edge. With the development of the docks between the wars along Southampton Water, vast qualities of chalk fill from Micheldever were deposited along the shore line to create the New Docks, or the Western Docks as it became known from 1965. With this and the building of the Civic Centre virtually over the tunnel, the centre of gravity of the city shifted westwards, thereby increasing the importance of the West Station, which was reconstructed and renamed yet again – bridges and the lines were quadrupled between the western tunnel portal and Millbrook, and a new station was opened, just west of the tunnel portal, as Southampton Central on 7 July 1934. The Blechynden levelcrossing was replaced by a new overbridge, and a junction into the docks was installed. The infrastructure at Southampton, unfortunately, made tempting targets for the Luftwaffe, Central station receiving its unwelcome attention on 22 July 1941, amongst other occasions.

As recorded in SW 23, during my early days in the New Works Drawing Office of the Chief Civil Engineer's Department at Waterloo, work had taken me to Bevois Park on several occasions, which sometimes involved a change of trains at Central station, during which opportunity would be taken to photograph the odd train or two. Subsequently a tour of the Permanent Way Works at Redbridge and photographic trips to Southampton Central were undertaken. My thanks to John Harvey for assistance in the matter of head codes.

*Opposite top:* **4-6-0 'Lord Nelson' Class No 30852** *Sir Walter Raleigh*, **built at Eastleigh in July 1928, with the 11.30am ex-Waterloo for Bournemouth slow on 31 January 1959 composed of Bulleid stock. No 30852 was withdrawn in February 1962. [35/21-17]**

*Opposite bottom:* **Maunsell 2-6-0 of the U Class, No 31795, was originally built by Armstrong Whitworth & Co in June 1925 as one of the ill-fated 2-6-4T K Class, No A795** *River Medway*. **Following the Sevenoaks disaster on 24 August 1927, in which sister engine No A800** *River Cray* **was derailed at speed, all were rebuilt as a 2-6-0 with a 3,500 gallon tender, No A795 in June 1928 at Eastleigh. It heads a goods train off the Bournemouth line on the afternoon of 31 January 1959. [35/21-18]**

*Below:* **On the same day, proud 'King Arthur' Class No 30782** *Sir Brian* **stands at the head of the Bournemouth to York train in Southampton station with clock tower in the background showing the time as 10.43am. No 30782 was built in July 1925 by the North British Loco Co and withdrawn September 1962. The leading coach is LMR porthole stock. [35/9-21]**

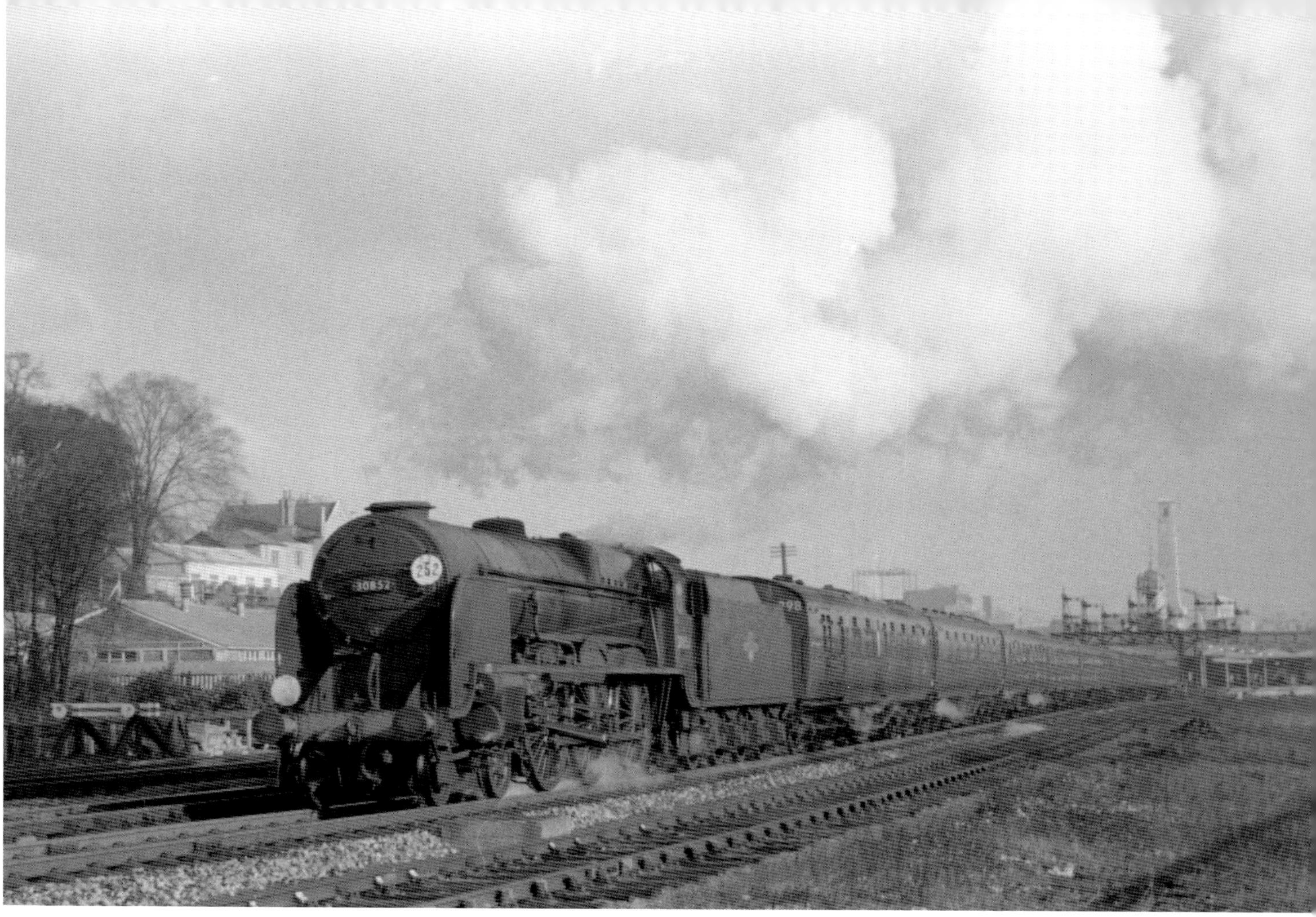
252
30852

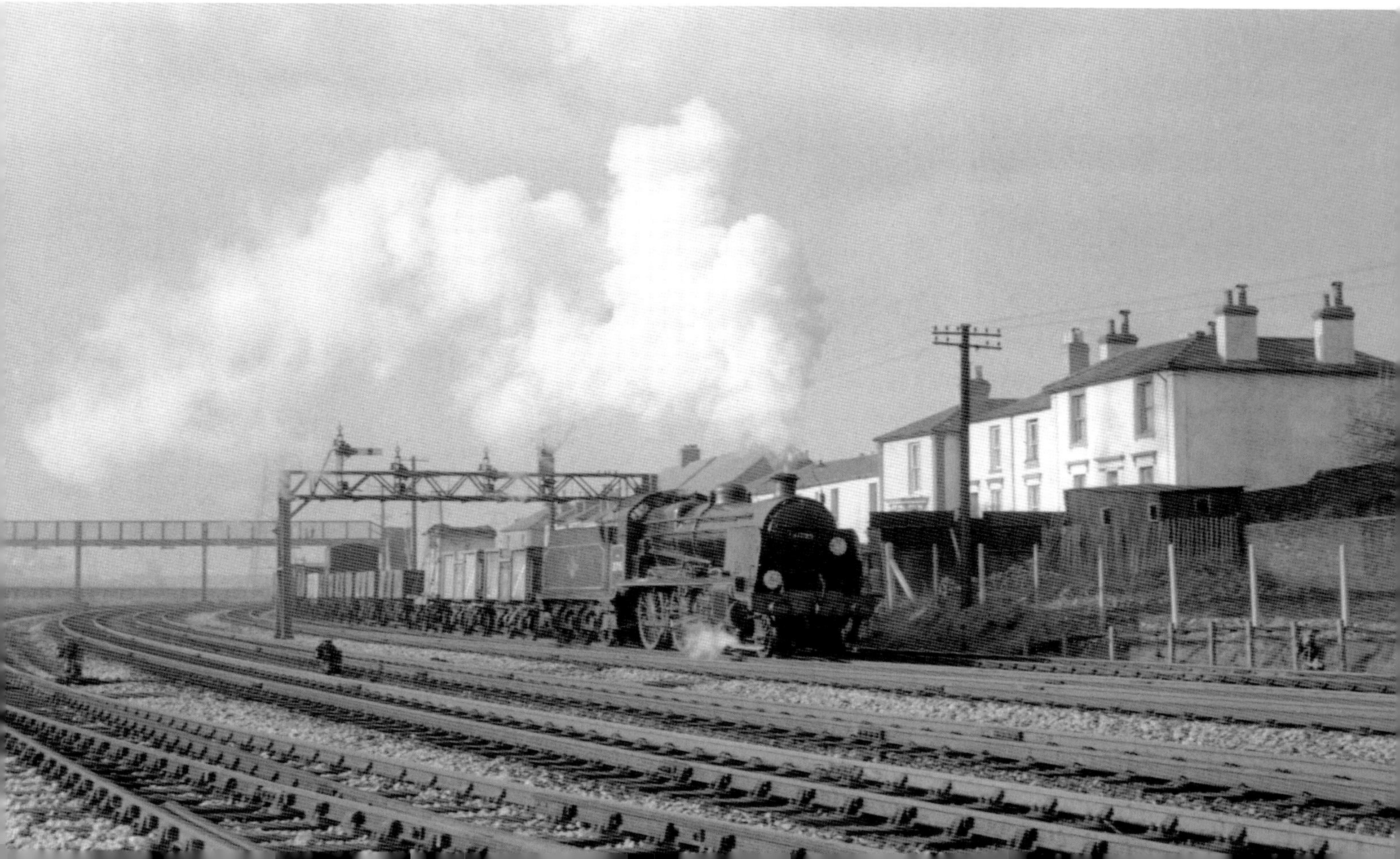

Sister engine No 31792, also built by Armstrong Whitworth & Co. in May 1925, was likewise rebuilt at Eastleigh in July 1928. The position of the lamps would suggest that this is a passenger train from Andover. [35/21-19]

Unrebuilt 4-6-2 'West Country' Class No 34007 *Wadebridge* with the 12.35pm Saturdays only from Waterloo to Bournemouth via Sway gets under way as it leaves Southampton Central station on a chilly but bright winter's day. [35/21-22]

During a visit to Redbridge Permanent Way Works on 22 December 1960 BR Standard 4-6-0 Class 4 No 75066 rushes through Redbridge station with a parcels train for Salisbury via the Romsey line. [35/38-22]

BR Standard 2-6-2T Class 3 No 82014 passes Redbridge Junction with a train of oil tank wagons from Fawley, two all steel end door mineral wagons leading to act as a barrier. [35/38-23]

LSWR built at Eastleigh in 1920, 4-6-0 'S15' Class No 30509 off the Romsey line drifts past Redbridge Junction with a permanent way train of Grampus wagons. [35/12-24]

## References:

Bradley D.L., *The locomotives of the South Eastern & Chatham Railway*, RCTS, 1961.

BR, SReg, Locomotives, Eastern Section, Diagram book.

BR, SReg, Locomotives, Western Section, Diagram book.

Dendy Marshall C.F., *A history of the Southern Railway*, The Southern Railway, 1936, pp 82, 114, 137, 645-651.

*Engine Head Signals*, Southern Railway, 1 January 1944.

Jackson, B., *Castleman's Corkscrew, Vol 1*, The Oakwood Press, 2007, pp 62, 95.

Jackson, B., *Castleman's Corkscrew, Vol 2*, The Oakwood Press, 2008, p108-109.

*Sectional Appendix to WTT*, Southern Region, Western Section, BR, 1 October 1960, p120-124.

Modified 'West Country' Class No 34017, still with its nameplate *Ilfracombe* and shield affixed and with a train for Bournemouth, takes water at Southampton Central while gently issuing steam from the safety valves on 14 July 1966. [35/70-2]

# Rebuilt
## The Letters and Comments Pages

I was asked the other day if there was any specific order to letters appearing in this section? Short answer – 'No', but I do try and put things in some sort of chronological sequence especially if they refer back to a much earlier edition of 'SW'; but otherwise it is very much a question of as it arrives – it gets added.

Starting then, from Michael Harvey of Crawley, reference **SW45** and **the illustration on p93.** 'The location is just south of Redhill. 'Redhill B' box being visible above the roof of the coaches. There are coal wagons in the gasworks siding whilst the passenger stock is in one of the sidings alongside the Reading branch. When I started at Redhill in 1958, Brighton – Redhill and return was worked by a Tonbridge 'L' which reached Brighton via Uckfield; and a Three Bridges crew. On Saturdays Brighton provided a 2-6-4T but it could well have been an Atlantic in earlier times.

**P48 (SW45)** 'Sandling may well be the same working – but a few years on – as the headcode also covered the Redhill-Tonbridge route. When Ramsgate shed closed in 1959 the 'Schools' class locos from there which had worked the trains were replaced by a 'Class 24'. At peak times the two sections were run as independent trains and the Redhill – Margate leg was often double-headed by two of these locos. In 1959 it was decided the train would no longer run during the winter months, it was then a surprise to find it restarting in 1960 and reverting to Schools class haulage again. The train could well be the Sussex part of the 7.35am Birkenhead cross-country which divided at Redhill. The main part served Ashford and the Kent coast, the Sussex portion of three-four coaches continuing to Brighton, Eastbourne and Hastings.'

*A recent find, courtesy of David Vaughan, was this view of Seaton Junction, which we would suggest was not long after its rebuilding in 1927/8. The view was taken from the Seaton branch train which has arrived at the junction and nestled up to three coaches possibly detached from a down Exeter working. Engine identification is a guess, LBSCR origin certainly, and possibly a D/D1? (No doubt somebody will give us a firm answer.) What would be equally interesting to know is the actual working and why the engine has ended up sandwiched as it is.*

From Jeremy Clarke re **SW46**. 'Hi Kevin, I think I may have an **answer to the puzzling headcode on p102**. As the oncoming train is at Oxted I think the code is basically Victoria to Tunbridge Wells West via Hever. It is unfortunate we have no date as this might elucidate things a little but I suggest this may be an extra or special working and the additional disc on the offside of the buffer beam could carry a note of its working number. For example, if this were a Ramblers' excursion it may be worked in passenger service only as far as Hever and go on empty to TWW for servicing. Such a working would appear in the weekly notices with the notifying number that applied to it, with that on the disc complying.

'As to **p26 (SW46),** the **'Ks' regularly worked to Salisbury on freight**. The fact that the caption comments on the presence of the leading vehicle as a loose coach and not in its allocated set would suggest to me that this is an ECS working to Clapham Junction whence the return of No. 32345 to its spiritual home would be straightforward.'

---

Now from Alastair Wilson with a question on **loco working on the Hastings line.** 'My family moved to Robertsbridge in 1947, and I lived there in the school holidays and on my leaves from the Navy until my marriage in 1957. Our farmhouse overlooked the northern approaches to Robertsbridge station, from the down outer home to the northern station limits. Like all right-minded boys of that era, I was a train-spotter with my 1947 Southern Railway *Ian Allan ABC*, in which I marked up my 'cops', using blue-black ink from my prized fountain pen – it was in the BB era, 'Before Biros'. (Sadly, I no longer have it – I wish I had.) I didn't have to haunt the station to do my spotting – I had a three-foot long Naval telescope, which had been my great-grand-father's; it had a three inch diameter lens at the front, and the magnification was such that I could read off the cabside numbers without too much problem at a range of about half-a-mile.

'The point of all this pre-amble is that I have been contemplating asking this question of my fellow-readers for some time, and, again, I seem to have got an answer, or partial answer, by chance. But I would like to have corroboration from someone else who can remember 'spotting' the ex-SECR Hastings line in that period. I 'copped' every type of ex-SECR and Southern 4-4-0s in use on the Eastern Section except D1s and E1s. I got one of the very last Stirling/Wainwright F1s on Tonbridge shed; I got one, maybe two, B1s on a local stopper; I got several Ds, likewise, I think. I got all the Ls, and several L1s, and every 'V' ('Schools') which were shedded at Bricklayers Arms or St. Leonards (the Ramsgate engines were very elusive). But never did I see a D1 or an E1. So I was going to ask our readership if they ever saw a D1 or E1 south of Tonbridge on a Hastings line train. I knew that they were largely used on the old Chatham route to Dover and Thanet, and on the South Eastern route to Reading, but I assumed that there must have been the odd one or two at 'the Arms', which could have ventured down to Hastings from time to time, and very suitable they would have been.

**Many readers will already be aware of the stunning collection of images taken by the late Edward Wallis depicting infrastructure, signalling and trackwork. Through the good offices of the Wallis family we have been privileged to be shown a number of 'new' views previously missing from the collection and which we can now show here for (we think) the first time in print. Starting here, we have a view of Exmouth – the station not the junction (although there is a junction here as well). Photographed from the top of the 'From Topsham home signal', we are looking towards the terminus and with the line arriving from Budleigh on the left. A very sharp curve allows passenger trains to approach the station or instead to continue straight ahead into the commodious goods yard. The date recorded for the image is 15 September 1928.**

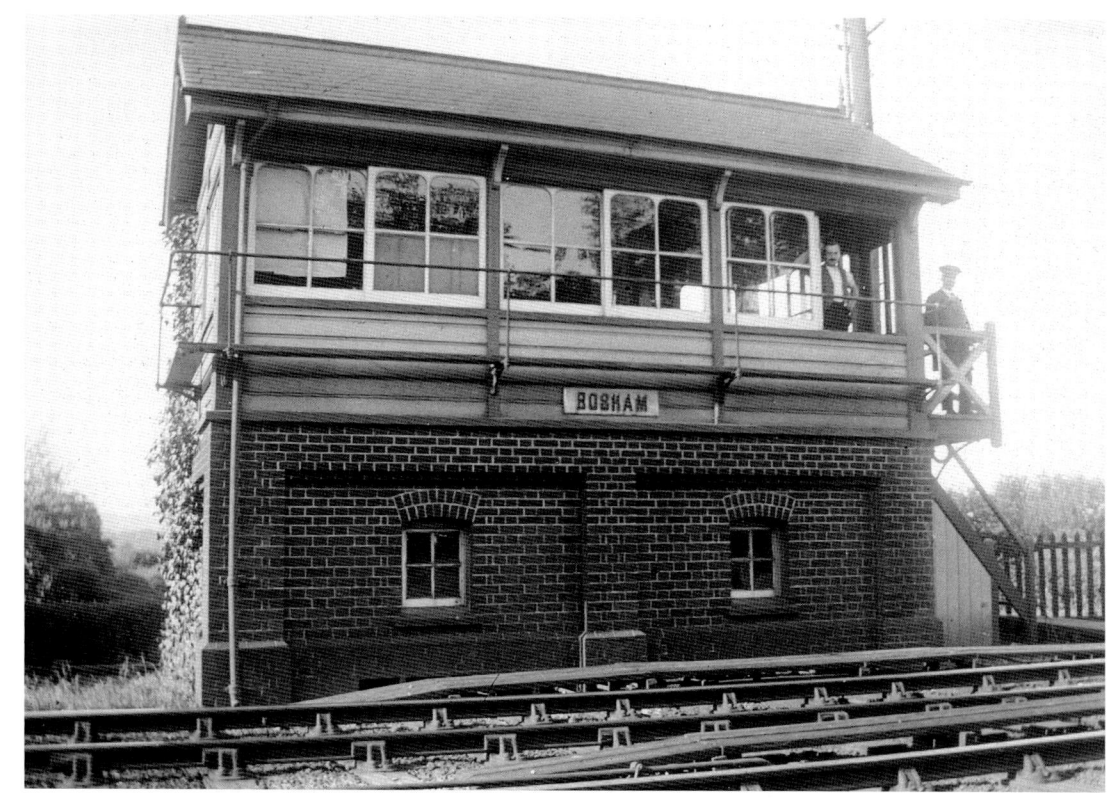

We move eastwards now to Bosham on the coastway line between Havant and Chichester. The signal box here also acted as a gate box for the adjacent level crossing. Within were 19 levers including No 15 which acted as an electrical release to Brook Lane Crossing GF, a short distance east towards Chichester. No date for when the view was taken.

'But this morning, I got an answer, in that in a new book I have just bought (one of the 'Pen and Sword' Locomotive Portfolio series, on the Maunsell 4-4-0s) there is an illustration, the only one I have ever seen, and in colour too, of an E1, No. 31507, at Wadhurst in 1958, with a train of 'blood and custard' Hastings line stock. This was the last summer of steam-hauled passenger trains, other than specials, and I wonder what the occasion was. The train looks to be six (two threes) standard Maunsell restricted width coaches followed by two more, the first of which could have been one of the third-class Pullmans which were included in two up and two down trains each weekday (normally they were formed in the middle of a seven coach train, so this would seem to have been a non-standard formation).

'So, does anyone have any record of a D1 or E1 on a scheduled Hastings service in the period 1947-57, or even on a hop-pickers' special from London to Robertsbridge?'

Alastair continues on the topic of **'Waller's Ash'** from **SW47**. 'I particularly enjoyed the piece by Stephen Duffell on the accident in 1842 in Waller's Ash tunnel, between Basingstoke and Winchester on the old LSWR main line. I go through it from time to time in a X-Country 'Voyager' these days, and will remember the five who died each time I go through it, on my way from Banbury to Southampton and Portsmouth.

'I made the following comments to myself as I read the article. Firstly, the Coroner's remarks about the jury selected for him by the Constable. I wrote: "Wow! He wouldn't half get stick for that, these days." I suspect, though, that in the days before any form of compulsory education, he might have had something of a point, though I also suspect that he probably underestimated the capabilities of the first-chosen jury. I would think the circumstances very similar to the modern call that there has been to do away with juries in complicated fraud cases, where laymen are deemed to be unlikely to be able to understand the financial complexity of the matter.'

'Shortly after that, the Coroner fairly let himself go on the shortcomings of the Constable, and I noted: "Poor old Constable – he got it in the neck, and no mistake. It was only a scant three years since a professional police force had been set up in Hampshire and quite probably the first time he'd had to do such a job, and there was probably no guidance – or very little – for him on how to proceed." And it's not good man-management to castigate a public servant in such a manner – the Constable's authority could be badly affected by such remarks.

'Finally, in footnote 1, with reference to 'deodands', I noted: "I believe that the other deodand referred to, of £1,000, probably referred to the accident on the GWR in Sonning Cutting on Christmas Eve, 1841 – some three-and-a-half months before the Waller's Ash accident, as a result of which the Coroner's jury put a deodand of £1,100 on the locomotive *Hecla* and the wagons of her train – there's a Wikipedia entry which describes it, but you'll find it in Hamilton Ellis's *Four Main Lines*, and in Macdermott, to give but two references. In that case the deodand was later overturned, and never paid – I would be interested to know if this one was paid, since Hamilton Ellis implied that deodands were abolished after the Sonning accident (though clearly the law hadn't been changed by April '42).'

From Graham Bowring, **Drayton/Portfield (SW45).** 'On page twelve I am fairly sure that the location is not Drayton but the next box to the west, Portfield. Assuming the caption to be correct in that it is a train from Brighton to Portsmouth, it cannot be Drayton as that box was on the up side with the platform next to it; none of which matches the photo. Right up to the 1970s when I lived at Havant, there were four intermediate boxes between Chichester and Barnham, in order in that direction: Whyke Road, Portfield, Drayton and Woodgate. At that time Portfield was the only one not at a level crossing, and quite near Whyke Road, so was only opened when a goods train needed to shunt the sidings. Back to the photo, I think the large building on the left looks like the factory later known as Bartholomews and was still served by train when I knew it. The Chichester bypass was built in 1937 and crossed the line by an overbridge just east of Portfield box making it an easy one to miss. The bridge is not in the photo but the factory is not on the 1933 OS map, so if I am correct about all this, the photo was taken between 1933 and 1937 (it has of course to be before 1938 when the line was electrified as there is no sign of the 3rd rail). By the way the box was originally named Portfield Ballast Pit; there were a lot of gravel workings in this area. Anyway, thanks for the chance for a bit of detective work!'

---

Now from Roger MacDonald on the subject of the **LSWR Locomotive Class Designations in SW 46**. 'This provides a useful reference, but there is one small correction to the table on page 8. Order D4 was not for Class T1 but for Class O2. Included in the order was none other than surviving O2 *Calbourne*. When she was stripped down for overhaul in 1992 and old paint was removed, a legend was uncovered behind the right driving wheel – '209 D4'. This was of course the original LSWR number and D4 was the works order number for this batch of the class. Having then survived 100 years, it was decided to carefully paint round and rewrite over the markings so that they can be seen by anyone peering behind the right driving wheel.'

---

And from Jeremy Clarke on the subject of his article on **the Croydon, Oxted & East Grinstead Railway in SW46** (the images for which were supplied by the office). 'Hi Kevin, mag arrived this morning thank you. Some really good historical illustrations but an inaccurate caption to the one on p93. It is the low level station at East Grinstead that remains in use and not the high level as implied here. I would not be surprised if this has already been pointed out by some readers. Thanks for making use of this.' (*I think others may have been too polite but a definite 'Mea-Culpa' from the office.*)

---

Now from Les Price and a caption correction to his article on the **Exeter Special** again in **SW46.** 'Just a note to say I received a copy of SW 46 from Crecy on Friday morning, thank you. It was a great pleasure to see my first article in print. Given that they were taken on a dull mid-winter day back in early 1966 you did a good job bringing the photographs up to publication standard. You may receive some correspondence from one or two of your more eagle-eyed readers! The location of the photo of *Exeter* on page 77 was actually Fareham, where we made a stop for the loco to take on water.'

---

Next a plea for help from our long term friend Rod Garner and his pet topic of **Torrington**. '"I gather from the SW editorial I have just quickly read through that the new abode is more rural and pleasant! Glad to hear it.

**No prizes here for recognising this as 'The Elevated Electric', the actual location being Thornton Heath. Of interest however is the triple dummy (read as – 'top to bottom left to right'), and the fouling bar on the inside of the rails immediately left. Each of the ground signals would rotate through 90° to show clear although it is interesting to see that the centre signal was designed to rotate clockwise compared with the ones above and below. Presumably this was to prevent a mechanical conflict? The actual structure is also both tiered and staggered, which may be noted by careful examination of the position of the tops of the lamp casings.**

'I am also prompted to write to see if you and/or your far more knowledgeable readers can assist with a signal box problem. As you know we are currently starting to rebuild the railway.

'We are attempting to restore/rebuild that which was there in operational days. This includes rebuilding the signal box, although as there's virtually nothing left of it, it will be an interesting job! A slight problem arises here, in that whilst we have some photographs, we have no drawings or plans and in spite of a lot of research cannot find any. It seems that Torrington might have been a 'one off'. It occurs to me that one of your followers may have some clues?' Rod can be contacted via the editorial office at the usual address of editorial@thesouthernway.co.uk

And from another kind supporter, Nicholas Owen. **'Might have beens'**. 'Talk of retrenchment with the SR Exeter line singling somehow reminded me of the opposite, the what-might-have-beens. The Hayes branch was once thought of as bearing right before the terminus and heading in the general direction of Biggin Hill; shades of the never-to-happen Southern Heights Railway. *That* was a Colonel Stephens project, which the old Southern Railway originally agreed to operate as an electric line, branching off between Selsdon and Sanderstead. And yet, south of Sanderstead towards East Grinstead, etc – as detailed in your latest issue (SW46) – never looked like being third-rail territory back before WW2. Among other non-starters was extension southwards of the good Colonel's Kent and East Sussex line. The Ouse Valley Line, heading south-eastward over a still-existing abutment just south of that wonderful viaduct, remained a mirage, as did hopes of pushing on beyond Caterham through the North Downs. And of course Leatherhead was never reached from Chessington South, though there are some glimpses of works done. You can blame Hitler for that. But I suppose we should thank the Kaiser for one railwaying thing. If WW1 hadn't intervened, the LBSCR would surely have started putting up overhead all over the place, including the main line to Brighton. Thank heaven for the much more sightly third rail.' (*Coincidence about the 'Boom or Bust' in this issue....! Ed.*)

From Nigel Tilly on the **Kent Coast and BEPs and CEPs**. 'I was somewhat late in getting hold of my copy of Issue 45, so I expect you have already received some help with the location of the photo on page 44, but, if not, here goes. I suggest it is on the section of line that was quadrupled between Rainham and Newington. If you look at Page 106 of the 1993 book *Kent Coast Heyday* (Ian Allan) you will find a P. Ransome Wallis photo taken at this location but looking in the opposite direction. (Inspection of your photo does indeed show that

**Gloucester Road and the East Croydon spur starting signal, again 'Elevated Electric' territory. No date, but certainly prior to 1927 as both arms are still painted red. Hence the distant arm has at its end a 'Coligny Welch' indicator – a fitting which showed a white chevron of light to the right of the coloured lens and which in shape resembled the notched shape of the actual arm. All three Southern constituents used this variation (not, it should be noted, on every distant signal) and which must have been a boon to drivers. (The only other company known to have adopted the fitting was the GER for use on certain of its signals within the London area.)**

```
                                    M

A.G.Pad. 270    12th September, 1927.

Dear Sir,
            Coligny-Welch Distinguishing Distant Signal Lamp.
                    The question has arisen as to the discontinuance of
the Coligny-Welch Signal Lamp in view of the revised requirements of
the Ministry of Transport, which provided that the distant signals
shall be distinguished from stop signals during daylight by yellow
coloured arms (fish tailed) and that at night such signals should
show a yellow light for the "caution" and a green light for the
"clear" position.

            I am informed that with the exception of a small
section of the London and North Eastern Railway, the Southern Railway
is the only one of the four Groups that has adopted this particular
type of lamp, and the recent decision to introduce the upper quadrant
type of semaphore would in any case necessitate a new type of marker
light being designed if it were to be continued.

                    Having been advised of the view of the various Of-
ficers concerned, I have come to the conclusion that the distinguish-
ing lights should be abolished in all new signals where the yellow
semaphore arms and lights are installed. Please arrange accordingly.
                                           Yours faithfully,
                                                     HAW
G.Ellson, Esq.,
    Engineer,
        Waterloo.
```

LNER 'A4' No 22 *Mallard* on the up line at Andover Junction during the 1948 interchange trials. Records show that this engine took part in an official trial in the down direction on 8 June (with the GWR dynamometer car) but was declared a failure at Exeter. A replacement 'A4' No 60033 *Seagull* arrived from King's Cross two days later and took part in down and up trials on 10 and 11 June respectively. Folklore has it that the choice of the Eastern Region in sending *Mallard* was based purely on the kudos the engine carried even though it was known not to have been in the best condition at the time. Possibly even a harassed ER official instructed to despatch an 'A4' deliberately sent No 22 in its known poor condition rather than a better performer. On the basis also that *Seagull* undertook up and down trials, we may reasonably conclude that the test of 8 June was not considered suitable. (SCT was involved in other aspects of the tests around this time with the reader referred to 'SW Special No 10' for further details.)

the sign has two faces.) The caption defines the location and gives a date of June 1958, which one might reasonably assume is also when your photo was taken. On a separate topic, the discussion of modifications to the BEPs and CEPs did not include anything on the 'air conditioning' of the buffet car of the final BEP, 7022. I remember getting into this on a very warm evening in the seventies and being immediately struck with how beautifully cool it was. I have seen it described more recently as "pressure ventilated" which surprised me as I would not expect this to have achieved the temperature reduction that I recall.

'So was this vehicle 'air conditioned' or 'pressure ventilated' and what was the origin of this experiment?'

As with the above and Rod Garner's request earlier, if you can add to the discussion we would be most grateful.

---

Thanks also to John Davenport, G. J. Ellis, and Graham 'Biggles' and Eric Youlden for letters also received.

# The Lost Archives of Stephen Townroe Part 13

*Above and overleaf:* **Restored and complete, No 563 stands outside the front of Eastleigh shed in light steam. We know A. B. McLeod was responsible for the final checks on paintwork and condition before the engine was released to the shed. It is seen here alongside at least two oil-burners, Nos 157 and 1625, one of the very few occasions on which they were recorded in steam at Eastleigh. SCT refers to Jack Francis also being present, possibly the man with the crew on the ground alongside the engine. What the role of Mr Francis was is not explained.**

Sometimes a picture can say a thousand words and the caption writer is left with the dilemma as to whether to point out the obvious or restrict any words to the factual, and information that might not be obvious from the image alone. (The reasons for this comment will become all too apparent a little later in this piece.)

Regular readers will recall that we left the last instalment of this selection with work having commenced on the stripping of No 563 at the start of its restoration. We commence this time with more on the resurrection of this engine which as we know came close to being scrapped, after which we have a Royal working and a 'Well Tank' fresh from overhaul. Most of the remaining views will be self-apparent or at least obvious from the captions.

But it is after the view of No 30585 that the point made in the first paragraph will become apparent and especially vis-à-vis the individuals concerned. We debated long and hard as to their inclusion but in the end they are reproduced – deliberately small – to indicate that whilst our railway interest may bring us satisfaction and for many employment, it could also be and remains to this day an extremely hazardous environment. In the case illustrated both men survived, we sincerely hope for many years after the event concerned.

61

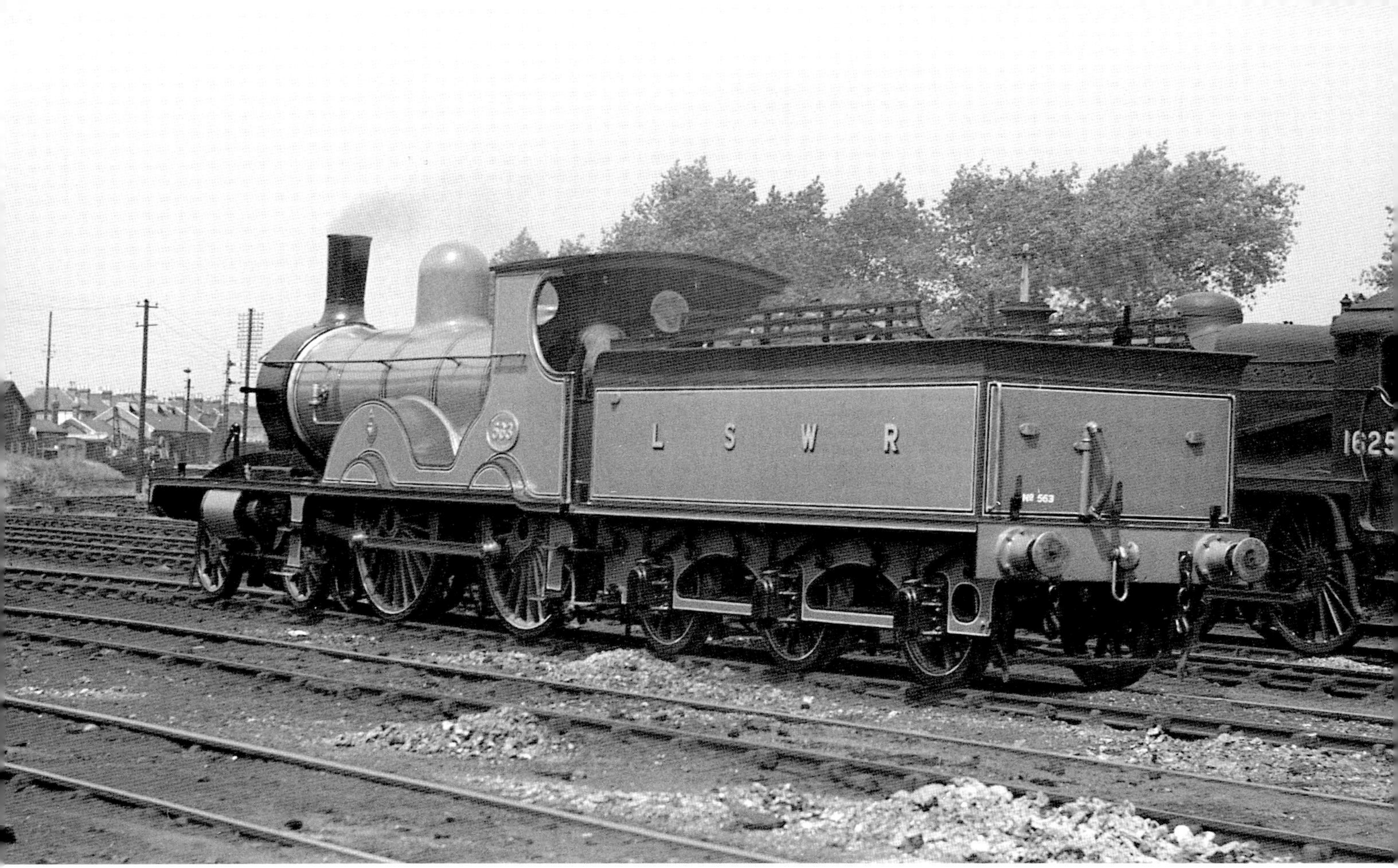
L S W R
No 563
1625

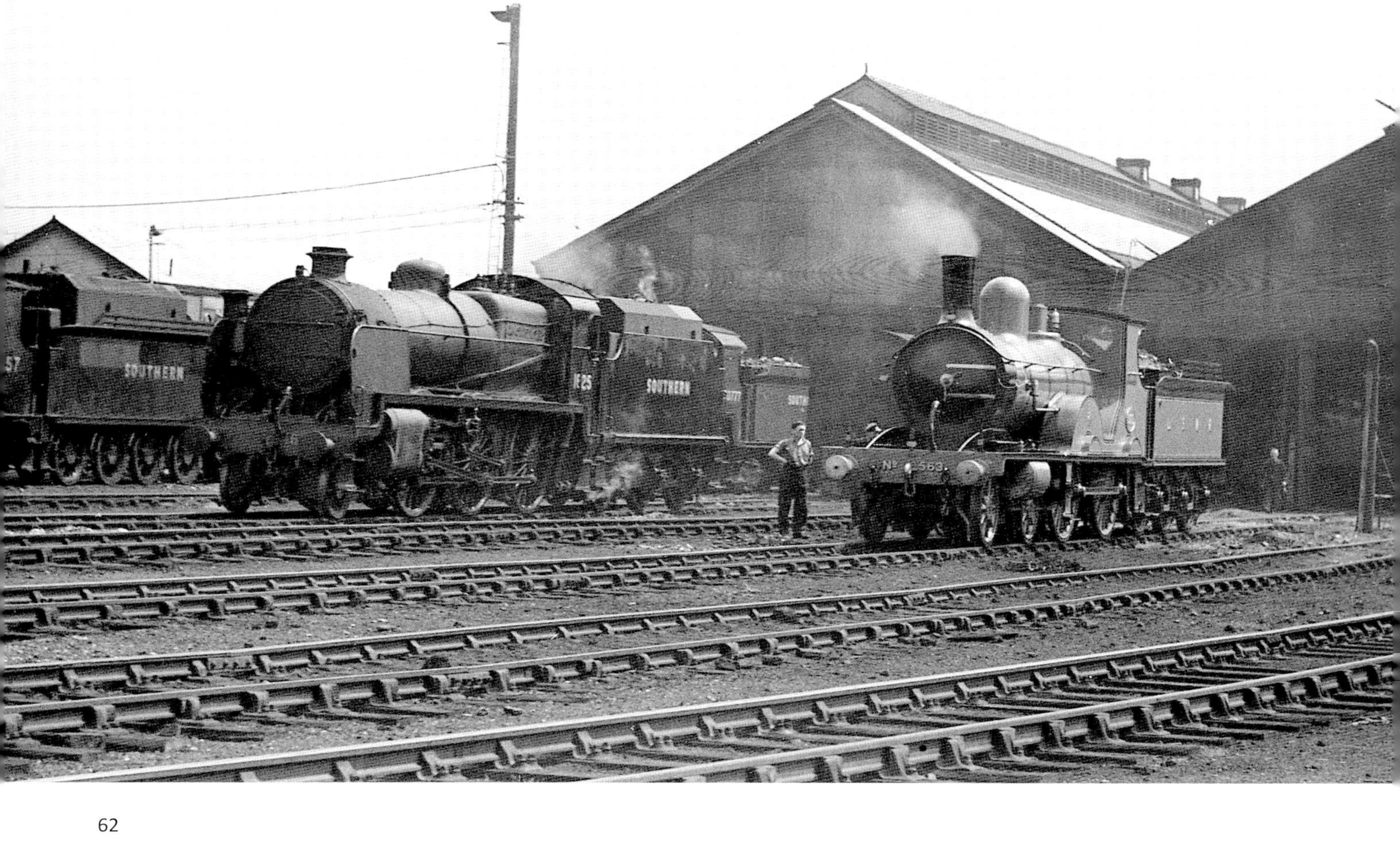
SOUTHERN
SOUTHERN
No 563

Cab view of No 563 most definitely in light steam. We know the boiler was not pressed to its original 175psi but at what lower limit the valves were set is not reported. As is known, the engine and a former LSWR coach restored at the same time were exhibited at Waterloo soon after, so was the 'T3' despatched under its own steam or towed? Likewise it would be interesting to learn if it undertook any trials from Eastleigh around this period.

No 30864 *Sir Martin Frobisher* at Southampton Docks on 28 July 1948 ready for a Royal working. Apart from the unnamed crew we know SR hierarchy in the form of Insp Langdon, Dr Hawkins, and Mr A. Earle-Edwards were also involved. The occasion was a visit of King George V1 and Queen Elizabeth to the Cunard lines *Queen Elizabeth*.

63

Coaling by steam crane at Eastleigh, the receiving loco 'N15X' No 32329 *Stephenson*. On occasions SCT would record several similar images of an incident or occasion but this time it is a solitary view and so we are left to wonder either if the coaling stage was temporarily out of use or if this was an experiment/necessity due to traffic requirements. No date is given.

In early BR livery and fresh from overhaul, we have this view of '0298' No 30585 fresh out of shops. Again the question may be asked, did the engine undergo a trial/brief period of running-in before returning to Wadebridge? We would assume that there must have been a trial of some sort, not least to confirm that a hot box or other issue might not occur on the 180-mile journey to its natural home.

The Lost Archives of Stephen Townroe Part 13

The images which were subject to debate at the start of this piece. The collapsed firebox of 'E4' No (3)2557 after the boiler explosion at Bevois Park sidings (Southampton) on 6 April 1949. Driver Cooper and Fireman Moors are also seen in hospital – fortunately both recovered. At 8.05pm the crew was shunting when the firebox of the engine burst inwards and both men were literally blown out of the cab, having sustained severe scalding. After the boiler had emptied and the steam subsided, examination revealed 137 of the 207 copper stays had broken, allowing steam pressure to bulge the copper side plate into the firebox and force it off the heads of the other 52 stays. Despite the pressure the plate itself did not fail, the hot steam and water escaping through the now 52 open stay holes. Subsequent examination revealed the actual copper stays to be badly corroded. The engine had been based at Eastleigh for just three weeks at the time, having spent the previous six years at Horsham, an area renowned for the corrosive properties of the water supply on copper. The boiler had been examined by an inspector four weeks earlier – while the engine was still at Horsham – and whilst noting that some of the stays had been attacked by corrosion, he considered it could run for a further six months. It was a terrible decision to have made. Repairs were subsequently made and as BR No 32557 the engine lasted in service until the end of 1962.

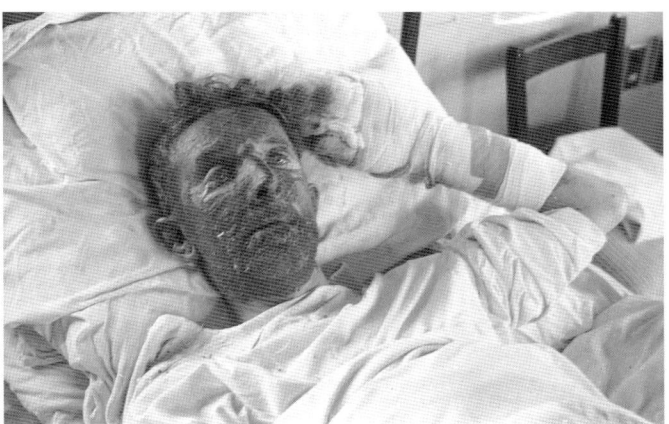

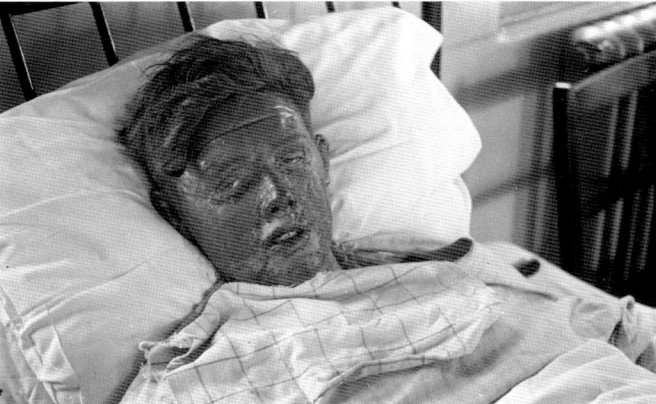

Two simple train views now, with a Urie 'H15', No 30478, leaving and an unidentified 'K10' both just west of Southampton Central. We are not told the purpose of these images and the index provided no further clue, possibly SCT just liked photographing trains!

The Lost Archives of Stephen Townroe Part 13

Next time in what will be the penultimate selection from *The Lost Archives'* series: tablet working on the Lymington branch, problems with the automatic tablet exchange on the Somerset & Dorset, train spotters, engines at speed and at rest, and scrapping of engines in March/April 1951.

On the footplate of a 'Nelson' on an 'Up' train and with Wallers Ash tunnel in the distance. This time we do have a sequence, this the first of four, with a similar image showing the approach to the tunnels at Micheldever, Popham and finally on the climb to Worting flyover. The engine is No 30853 *Sir Richard Grenville*.

Finally for this instalment we have some images inside Eastleigh Works. The first three were taken, according to SCT's list, around July 1949 and show the final 'Merchant Navy' Pacific, No 35030 *Elder Dempster Lines*, in the process of assembly. The date though has to be questioned slightly as previously published records refer to the same engine having been completed in April. Whatever, one fact we cannot dispute is that this was the final member of the class to be built although Eastleigh would build further Bulleid engines in the form of some 'Light Pacifics' after this date. The very last image is a set of wheels from a Maunsell/Urie 4-6-0, the frames for which are probably those alongside. The detritus of a typical railway workshop lies cluttered around – the number of trip-hazards alone is almost impossible to count – but then this was a typical workshop from the period.

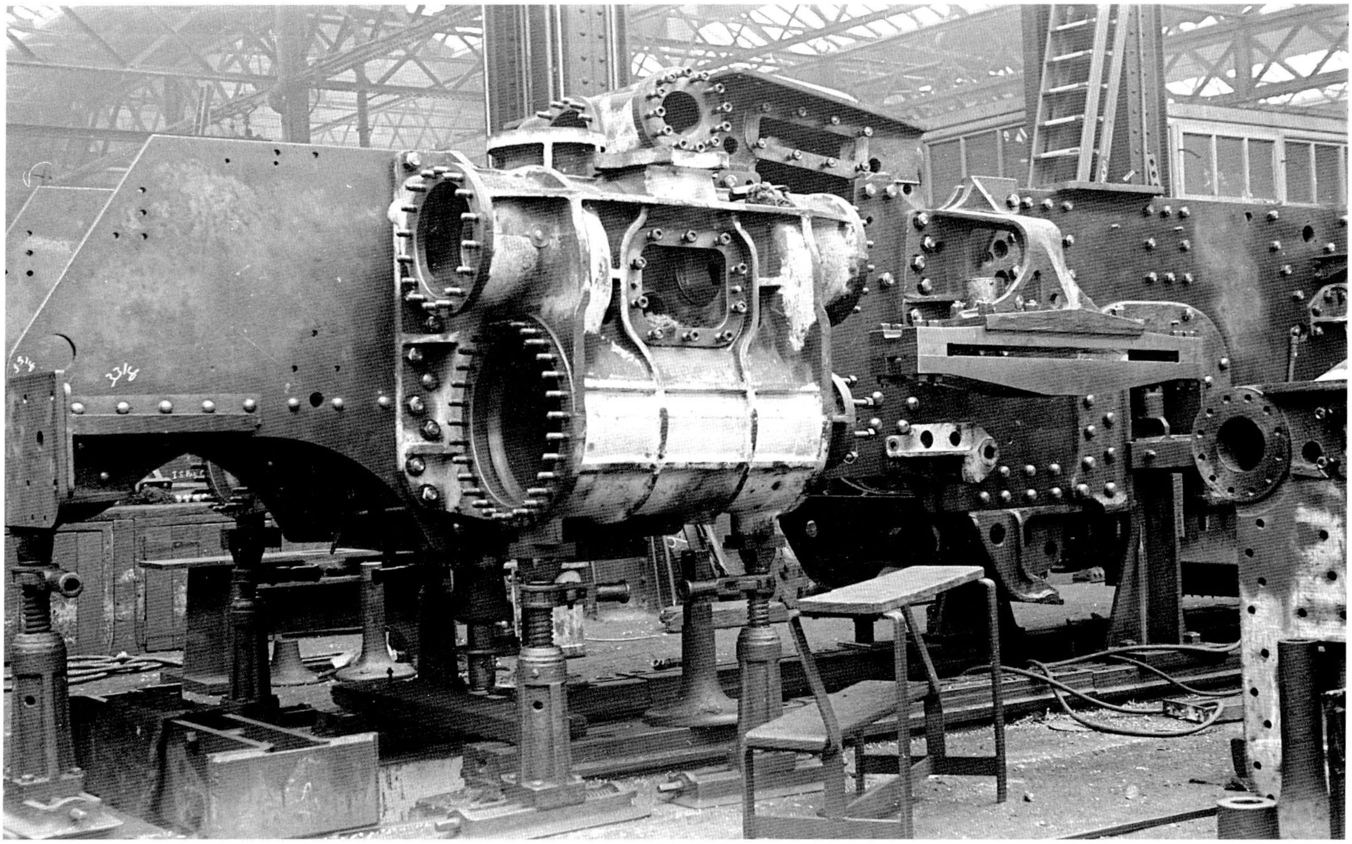

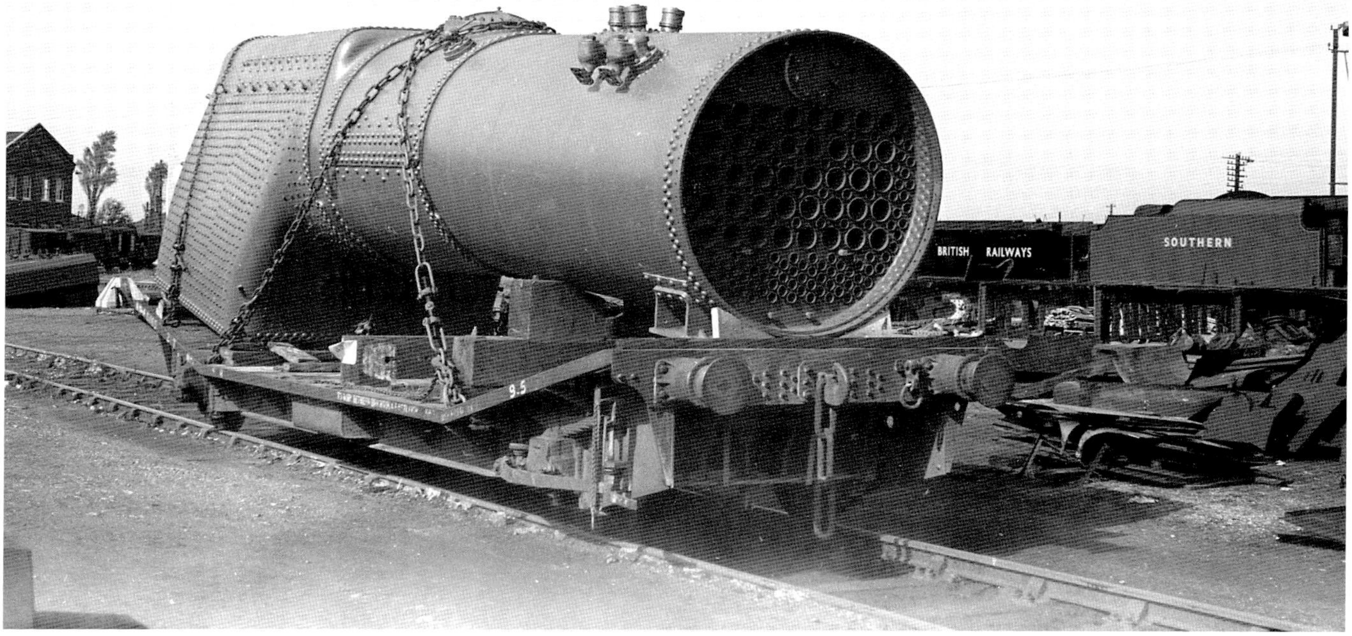
BRITISH RAILWAYS
SOUTHERN

The Lost Archives of Stephen Townroe Part 13

69

# Interlude at Penshurst, 1966

## Les Price

The scenes illustrated in these photographs have now disappeared entirely. The station became unstaffed in 1967, very shortly after the last photograph was taken. In line with other stations along the route, the main buildings on the 'up' side were subsequently demolished in 1971. The Dutton & Co signal box of 1893 was decommissioned on 5 March 1986 with the introduction of colour light signalling. In 1993 the line was electrified and services began to run through to London rather than Reading. The 'down' staggered platform was demolished and an entirely new platform constructed, directly opposite the old up platform which itself was completely rebuilt. At the same time the old sleeper footcrossing adjacent to the signal box was removed and replaced by a footbridge. *(All images by the Author)*

*Above:* **Under the watchful eye of a solitary waiting passenger, 'Tadpole Unit', No 1204 runs into the staggered 'Down' platform at Penshurst. This set was working the 8.24am service from Reading to Tonbridge. Penshurst station, on the old SER main line, had opened on 26 May 1842. Although situated in the village of Chiddingstone Causeway, the station was given the soubriquet due to its proximity to Penshurst Place, one of England's grand houses but some two and a half miles to the south. Naming stations like this was a ploy used by Victorian railway builders to appease and encourage the local gentry. 26 April 1966.**

*Opposite bottom:* **The driver of unit No. 1314 ex Reading train gazes back down the platform at penshurst whilst awaiting the 'tip' from the Guard in order to resume his journey to Tonbridge. These sets shared duties with the Tadpole sets, (Nos. 1201 to 120' officially Class '3R' Diesel-Electric Multiple Units. Nicknamed 'Tadpoles', the name stuck and was later officially adopted by the Southern Region. The abandoned goods shed behind the trains still appears in sound condition despite withdrawal of goods services at the station from 9 September 1963.**

*Above:* **Despite slowing for its Penshurst call, this unidentified 'Tadpole Unit' forming the 1.48pm ex-Tonbridge to Reading service still continues to spew diesel exhaust into the atmosphere as it enters the deep cutting on its approach to the station. By 1964, as the route carried relatively few passengers, new trains could be justified. The answer was to take twelve carriages from Class 201 'Hastings Units', then surplus to requirements, together with six redundant driving trailers from 2-EPH EMUs and form them into six 3-car units. 26 April 1966.**

Sunday evening at Penshurst. A Birmingham R.C.W.Co Type 3 Bo-Bo Diesel-Electric (Crompton) No D6513 cautiously approaches its stop with the 5.5pm Redhill to Tonbridge passenger train. This was in fact a combined working of passenger and parcels stock comprising some eleven vehicles. It would have required an experienced driver to pull the train up precisely with the two/three passenger vehicles at Penhurst's small 'Down' platform. 8 May 1966.

Blasting exhaust into the air, the same train is seen departing. The second vehicle has a working designation permanently inscribed almost in WR style but it is unfortunately not possible to discern from the negative. D6513 subsequently became No 33102, was preserved and, following restoration in 2012, is now operational on the Churnet Valley Railway in Staffordshire and carries the name *Sophie*.

Diverted via Redhill owing to engineering work on the direct line, 'Hastings' unit No 1019 forming the Sunday 4.39pm Hastings – Charing Cross emerges from the cutting east of the station and goes full-tilt through Penshurst. Dominating the scene is the tower of St Luke's Church, Chiddington Causeway, built in 1898. The community itself grew around the railway station and with the development of the cricket bat and ball industry.

'Tadpole' unit No 1201, forming the Sunday 6.48pm Tonbridge – Redhill service, drifts into Penshurst. Apart from the tracks, the rest of the scene has been totally eradicated and transformed with the introduction of third-rail electrification, a new platform built so these are now opposite each other and basic shelters have replaced the former buildings. Annual passenger figures for 2017/18 indicate 34,854 used the station during the period, a drop from a peak of 41,832 two years earlier.

Guard Tom Price (Salop), whilst on a visit to his son in Chiddingstone Causeway, watches the arrival of the 7.24am Reading to Tonbridge as it runs into Penshurst about 9.40am. The train is formed of a Class 205 'Hampshire' 3-car unit No 1115, affectionately (or otherwise) known as 'Thumpers'. Built at Eastleigh in 1957 as one of the original batch of the class, it was initially employed on services in Hampshire but was initially employed on services in Hampshire but was subsequently transferred to the Central section to replace the ageing 'Tadpoles' on the Reading to Tonbridge service. Penshurst signal box, on the right, continued in use until the line was electrified in 1993. 8 April 1967.

# Len Mumford
## A Railway Life
### Michael Rowe

**Unfortunately minus headboard, an unidentified 'Squadron' has charge of the down 'Bournemouth Belle' at Woking.** *Peter Knottley*

When I was a child and budding railway enthusiast, my mother would proudly state that railways were in my blood. The pride with which she made that statement stemmed from the source of that blood, her father. I suppose these days we would state with greater appropriateness that railways are and have always been part of my DNA.

I have many childhood memories of travelling on the Southern Region with my grandfather. Excursions to the coast at Brighton and Hastings, with the latter also a venue for family holidays for which a trunk was sent on ahead by rail to the hotel. Family outings to Esher for Sandown Park racecourse were also regular events. My mother's younger brother lived in Oxted and we would visit him and his family, catching the steam-hauled East Grinstead and Uckfield services from Victoria which chugged through the North Downs via Riddlesdown and Woldingham. Then there was an aunt, or in my case a great-aunt, who lived near Woking. Whether before or after he retired, riding the railways with my grandfather enabled me to share and absorb his great love of the railway life and I benefited from the access to people and places his lifetime's service afforded him.

Whether it was sitting on his knee on the platform at Woking, no more than seven or eight years old, awaiting the progress of the up *Bournemouth Belle* whose approach had been announced by the distant whoop of its pilot's whistle and then experiencing the fearsome surge of a Bulleid Pacific rocking and clanking towards us, the exhaust of grey and white steam engulfing us as the rake of chocolate and cream Pullman cars rattled by, or him introducing me to the nooks and crannies that lay beneath Waterloo Station which were concealed from the millions of commuters using the great station; such experiences planted the desire to explore and experience the many wonders of the railway – the old LSWR main line in particular – which have endured for a lifetime.

Len Mumford

He could and did open doors for me that remained closed for my other train-mad school friends. Only twice did I walk through the entrance gates at Nine Elms Shed rather than climb over a wall from an adjoining building in Thessaly Street; one was on 9 July 1967, the last day of steam operation on the Southern Region, by when no one cared who was on the premises, and the other was when my grandfather arranged an official visit. Although by then retired, he had known the shed-master Mr Gilchrist for many years and after a brief reunion in the head man's office, we were given the run of the running sheds and yard.

Leonard Mumford was LSWR through and through. His family hailed from Chobham near Woking, within spitting distance of that company's main line from Waterloo to Basingstoke and beyond, although he spent much of his childhood on the Isle of Dogs, living with a relative who ran a corner shop. Although I have no specific knowledge, my understanding has always been that 'Len' was not a first generation railway man, there having being other members of the family who plied their trade in what he always referred to as 'The Service'.

Len joined the London & South Western Railway in 1909, at the age of fifteen. To be precise he became a booking clerk in one of the six signal boxes that then controlled the approaches to Waterloo Station. Over the next quarter of a century he spent the majority of his time acquiring the skills of a signalman, eventually being promoted to the rank of Leading Signalman in November 1936. The majority of that time was spent working in the old Waterloo 'A' Box, which in typical LSWR style traversed the tracks to the south of the terminus, a short distance from the end of the platforms.

I inherited from my grandfather a collection of photographs including several of 'A' Box, which not only show its location, but also the interior. Some of these portraits include Len standing by his section of the frame, in shirt sleeves with his trousers secured by taut, broad braces and with a cigarette balanced on his lower lip. Alongside are his colleagues, similarly attired, all of them posing for the photographer. Despite the careful choreography there is a sense of alertness as if a block and bell might ring at any moment, requiring a train movement to be facilitated with the routine efficiency Len expounded to me over many years. Trains approaching the great terminus should not be delayed because the platform into which they were to be received had not yet been vacated; empty stock movements should always be conducted with expedition, so as not to cause a logjam.

**Waterloo Cricket Club, 1911. Winners of The Drummond Challenge Cup. Len Mumford is third from the left in the middle row.**

**A view of 'A' Box taken from the approach to a surprisingly empty and quiet Waterloo Station.**

As I compose this essay, on my worktop stands the crown of the handle of one of the levers shown in those photographs of 'A' Box, severed as a memento when the box was closed and dismantled, and which I employ as a paperweight. That decapitation occurred in 1936, the year of Len's promotion to leading signalman, which coincided with the opening of the new electric box, which for the next fifty years stood on the north side of the tracks outside Waterloo, set squarely above Westminster Bridge Road. The opening of this installation was a considerable step forward, both in terms of technological development and working conditions for its staff. The only disconcerting aspect, or so it seemed to the author when as a lad of between ten and fifteen he made several visits to Waterloo Box, was the lack of any alternative access save for crossing the tracks from the end of platform 21, negotiating the approaches to the North Sidings and avoiding the live third rails. This always seemed an unnecessary series of risks, particularly if there was one or more M7 or Standard tank locomotives lurking in the sidings, awaiting their next duty to haul a string of empty stock to Clapham Yard.

By 1936 it was clear Len was a conscientious and dedicated company man. The 'Company' was no longer the LSWR, but since 1923 the Southern Railway. His career was about to develop rapidly, but he had already established a reputation for reliability and the application of common sense. He was also someone who was keen to engage with his work colleagues. That remained the case until shortly before his death many years later, following a lengthy retirement. Len was for several decades until shortly before he died in 1977 the chairman of the Brunswick House Institute and Club, which provided facilities for rest and recreation for Southern Region employees. That organisation operated from a fine, listed, Georgian building of the same name, which is still located a short distance from Vauxhall Station. The building is now dwarfed by the many tower blocks constructed around it along the south bank of the Thames, but can still be glimpsed from the main line as up trains approach Vauxhall. I attended several functions at Brunswick House during my early youth and as the years passed played snooker with Len in the 'Club's' splendid billiard room.

Len was also a keen cricketer. He loved sport and while – no doubt because of his boyhood years on the Isle of Dogs – he supported Millwall Football Club, there was never any doubt cricket came first in his sporting affections. We know he joined the Waterloo Station Cricket Club as soon as he joined the LSWR. There is a photograph of the victorious team for the 1911 season, which won the Drummond Challenge Cup. It was taken on the emerging concourse of the construction site for the new station, probably adjacent to platforms seven and eight. Len, who stands third from left in the middle row, was seventeen and is not the only young member of the team, there being two other youths of a similar age in the same row.

Len first met Lillian, my grandmother, while playing for Waterloo Cricket Club at Ashtead, Surrey, and his love of cricket was passed down the generations to me. Len and Lillian, whom he married in 1919, lived in an estate of Edwardian flats on the Kennington side of Walworth Road, where my parents also lived in the same block. It was only ten minutes' walk to the Oval Cricket Ground and I spent many days watching Surrey and England during my childhood, often with Len. He would recall great matches from the so called 'Golden Age', the autumn of which he had witnessed and his particular hero was Jack Hobbs, who he referred to as 'The Master'. Len said Jack had the fleetness of foot of a ballet dancer and told how if he was on early turn in 'A' Box, often the relieving shift would arrive having spent the morning at The Oval and announce 'The Master's batting', which would inevitably mean Len's journey home on the Northern Line would not end at Kennington, but would continue to Oval, where he would then spend several hours watching the cricket.

**The interior of 'A' Box with Len Mumford second from the camera on the left.**

**Another interior view of 'A' Box, this time with Len nearest the camera, cigarette in mouth.**

One final cricketing connection; at the foot of my grandparents' bed throughout my childhood stood a wooden chest, which on its lid has the inscription 'Waterloo ACC'. I believe this was the coffin in which the stumps, pads, bats and balls used by Waterloo Station Cricket Club were once stored. The chest is now in one of my garden sheds, still serving a useful purpose more than a century after it was first knocked together.

As WW2 approached with all the political uncertainties then current, Len's career began to progress. In December 1937 he was promoted to Yard Inspector. As the War began he therefore acquired further and wider responsibilities at Waterloo, which would lead to the most distinguished period of his service.

I grew up sharing numerous visits to his former workplace, sometimes specifically for our mutual pleasure with Len returning to his beloved temple and me engrossed with the

*Right:* **Len (left) with Mr Greenfield in the new Waterloo Signal Box circa 1936. The gentleman on the right is not identified.**

*Below:* **Damage to main line arches 160, 161 and 162 on the approach to Waterloo 7-9 September 1940.** *Spence Collection*

exploration of the great terminus with the attendant visceral pleasures that engaged my senses. The hiss and smell of steam beneath the broad grime-stained glass roof, the noise of the constantly changing congregation traversing the concourse, the rattle of the destination and arrival boards, which clicked and clacked as the lists of stations emerged and then disappeared, and the constant announcements made by a woman whose clear cut-glass voice carried absolute authority as she gave the same degree of importance to announcing the imminent departure of the 1226hrs to Hampton Court from platform 1, as she did to the 1230hrs *Bournemouth Belle* from platform 11. Len, of course, knew her very well, although I have long forgotten her name.

To me as a small boy heading towards his teenage years, Waterloo was akin to a vast cathedral, with its crypts and cloisters, tunnels and passageways, Len's tales of his exploits during the Blitz and then later, in the summer of 1944 when the V1 flying bombs rained on London and Waterloo in particular, etched vivid images in my consciousness, which have endured for a lifetime.

The South London in which I grew up was still scarred and pock-marked with bomb-sites and streets that no longer led anywhere. Listening to Len and my parents, I could imagine those districts in the immediate aftermath of a bombing: crowded with fire trucks and ambulances, the ruined houses and tenements smouldering: their stunned occupants standing or sitting in the rubble as the emergency crews went about their routine responses to the nightly terror wrought by the bombers. Len told me of the mornings when he was on early turn and the Northern Line was not running, so he walked the mile or so from Kennington to Waterloo, his route regularly changing due to the fires and destruction caused by enemy action. He had to step through the wreckage of broken buildings and over deflated hoses; exchanging words of encouragement with those tending to the survivors while he inhaled a toxic cocktail of dust and fumes. Len told me the sudden disappearance of familiar landmarks, buildings or places which had been a staple component of his existence was something that never failed to shock him.

He had also told me of how during WW1, as a young man in a reserved occupation, he had spent night shifts perched on the roof of Waterloo Station watching for Zeppelin airships. His experience during the Blitz of 1940 and 1941 was far more immediate and dangerous. In short, Len took to walking the tracks between Waterloo and Vauxhall, looking for bomb damage. He would set off from the end of a platform, shortly after the sirens sounded, walking slowly through the black out. He recalled how his eyes would adapt to the total darkness, which was only relieved by search light beams criss-crossing the sky, the distant flashes of anti-aircraft guns – there was a large battery on Clapham Common – and the blasts and resulting fires caused by falling bombs. Sometimes those explosions were uncomfortably close to the viaduct over which the tracks in and out of Waterloo run. Occasionally there was a direct hit on the railway; finding the location and extent of the damage was his objective.

Several times he achieved just that. One night at the beginning of the Blitz he was alerted that a signal had changed to red as a consequence of the circuit being broken. Close to Vauxhall, Len suddenly became aware the ground in front of him appeared darker than before which caused him to stop. He briefly turned on his torch and realised he was standing on the edge of a large crater, a high explosive bomb having crashed through the permanent way into the structure below. He quickly made his way to the nearest signal gantry to use the telephone and raise the alarm. He told a reporter from *The Star* (one of London's three evening papers, when interviewed upon his retirement in 1959): 'There was no advance evidence of a huge hole. The bomb blew everything out underneath, but caused no extensive surface damage.' On this occasion Waterloo was shut for almost two weeks while the damage was repaired.

There were other occasions when he and his companions reported damage to the tracks, or railway infrastructure. Another duty, particularly on the return leg of a patrol, was to remove unexploded incendiary bombs from the tracks and sidings. These were typically dropped in baskets, their descent sometimes slowed by small parachutes and upon landing they would ignite and collectively start a series of fires. These were a particular threat to Waterloo itself with the broad planes of glass panels spread across its roof. The railwaymen collected these dangerous munitions and handed them over to the police or army. Some were kept as souvenirs; it was only in 2017 my family finally handed to the Metropolitan Police a bomb Len had brought home from work one morning in 1941.

An anecdote Len told me about these regular nocturnal adventures was offered in response to my enquiry as to what would happen if we accidentally touched the live third rail while crossing the tracks to Waterloo Box. He told me how one night during the Blitz, close to the end of Platform 1, his foot had carelessly glanced against the live rail and he had been catapulted into an adjacent bunker containing sand. Throughout the twenty-five years I knew Len, he was always smartly turned out and I have cherished the thought of him, stunned and disarrayed, clambering out of that bunker. I have to admit I always retained doubts about the veracity of that story, but I do hope it was true.

Another wartime event which both Len and my mother recounted concerned an incident in June 1944 when a V1 flying bomb crashed on the north side of Waterloo Station, destroying track and rolling stock in the Windsor line platforms and causing damage to the offices in the block between platforms 15 and 16, which was where the station master and his staff were located. Len told me he was walking across the main concourse on his way to those offices when the bomb struck and he was blown off his feet. My mother was working as a secretary for Jeffreys, a company with offices a short distance away in Waterloo Road, and she and her colleagues had heard the bomb's engine cut out and were rushing down the stairs to shelter in the basement when the blast occurred. It was soon confirmed Waterloo had been hit and during her lunch break she walked the short distance to the station to establish that Len had not been injured. The station was closed

**Damage to station and stock, platforms 3 and 4 at Waterloo, taken at 8.04 pm 15 October 1940.** *Spence Collection*

so she was not certain he was safe until both of them arrived home from work that evening.

Len's conduct during the Blitz did not go unnoticed. On 16 May 1941 the Traffic Manager of the Southern Railway, Mr R. M. T. Richards, wrote to Len Mumford in the following terms: 'My attention has been drawn to the splendid courage, initiative and devotion to duty repeatedly displayed by you during air raids in London, and I desire to express my high appreciation of your fearless conduct and to inform you that the exceptional services you rendered under conditions of great danger have been under consideration by the Committee appointed to submit recommendations for Awards in connection with meritorious conduct and initiative shown by members of the Southern Railway Staff at personal risk to themselves. It will give me pleasure to arrange for the result of the recommendation of the Committee to be communicated to you in due course.'

Mr Richards wrote again in January 1943 to express his 'great pleasure' at learning Len had been awarded the British Empire Medal in the New Year's Honours List. The investiture by the King took place on 13 April 1943. When I started collecting train numbers in the early 1960s Len told me it was Ian Allan, then working in the Southern Railway's publicity department, who took him to have his official photograph taken. My train-spotting friends were suitably impressed that my granddad had met the man whose books we all eagerly purchased.

It was not only Len's bravery that was rewarded in 1943. In August that year he was promoted to Second Class Inspector and the following February he was appointed Assistant Station Master at Waterloo. Although he would subsequently become a station master in his own right, I always perceived that Len considered the five years he held this post to be the zenith of his railway career. A cutting kept by my late grandmother,

The Southern Railway publicity photograph organised by Ian Allan in February 1943, after Len was awarded the British Empire Medal.

presumably taken from an internal Southern Railway magazine, or newssheet, provides a report of what it describes as 'A pleasant little gathering', which took place in Waterloo Box on 29 February 1944. Len was presented with a case of pipes, tobacco pouch and tobacco by Leading Signalman G. O. Moseley, who tendered the opinion that, 'Mr Mumford was at all times ready to help the men and they had no hesitation in appealing to him for advice and assistance.' Mr Moseley is said to have been supported by other Inspectors, the signalmen, Yard Foremen, permanent way staff, and Signal and Telegraph department. In reply Len is reported to have thanked 'all concerned' and reflected that he had spent, 'many happy years in the Box.'

This latest promotion brought him into even closer proximity with a man he held in the highest regard and with whom he remained on close terms for the remainder of their joint lives. The Station Master at Waterloo during the Second World War was Mr Greenfield. I have not been able to ascertain his forename. As is immediately apparent from several photographs I inherited from Len, Mr Greenfield (as Len always called him) was an impressive and substantial individual. In one of his photographs he is standing alongside a locomotive with two colleagues, wearing his frock coat and top hat. He has signed the photograph in green ink, as I suppose a good Southern man would do, almost as if it is an item of memorabilia to be handed to a fan.

The warmth of the relationship between Len and Mr Greenfield is illustrated by a letter the latter sent to Len on 31 March 1942. It is headed '50 Glorious Years' and is an effusive acknowledgement of a gift tendered by Len to mark the passing of that milestone by his superior. Mr Greenfield states, 'It is most unusual for any Station Master, especially one controlling so large a station as Waterloo, to have the respect and esteem of the signalling staff and its supervisors...' In relation to Len personally, his superior goes on to record his gift will be:

'"Treasured throughout my remaining days as a lasting tribute from one who, no matter how hard and under what circumstances, whether adverse or otherwise, has stuck loyally to me. Since my arrival at Waterloo in 1925 I have always had the greatest respect and confidence in your ability and have profited by your sound judgment and common sense, and can honestly say it has been one of the pleasures of my life to have known you.'

It does appear there was longstanding mutual appreciation between these two railwaymen, both of whom were born in late Victorian Britain and served their apprenticeships in the pre-grouping era. No doubt Mr Greenfield was instrumental in Len's advancement at Waterloo and Len always spoke of him as if he was royalty. Indeed, I did meet Mr Greenfield at a function at Brunswick House in the mid-1960s, when Len presented, rather than merely introduced, me to his former boss. I recall an ageing but still formidable presence.

Len did meet royalty during his period as Assistant Station Manager. On several occasions he greeted the Queen (later Queen Elizabeth the Queen Mother) as she returned to London from official appointments. He said she was very gracious and my mother always commented the Queen without fail remembered his name. She would become irritated when her son pointed out that doubtless Her Royal Highness would have been briefed by her staff shortly before arrival who was on duty and receiving the royal train.

As a footnote to these royal contacts, when in 1965 the Queen and Duke of Edinburgh returned from their first state visit to West Germany, they arrived back in London at Platform 11, Waterloo Station, and Len and his family were among the reception party. Although Len had by then been retired for six years, he still had numerous contacts, not least through Brunswick House. Somehow Len, my grandmother, my parents and me found ourselves positioned behind a barrier on the platform adjacent to the point at which the Queen and Prince Philip would alight, be greeted by the Prime Minister Harold Wilson and then walk to the adjacent (and now long defunct) cab road, where her limousine awaited. My recollection is that there were no security checks or searches. I think Len, having cleared our attendance with a contact, simply made himself known to whoever was in charge of the railway aspects of the operation and we were shown to our positions among the small, apparently far from select, group of loyal subjects assembling in anticipation of the arrival of the royal train. We were facing towards the buffers and platform 10 was also vacant. I believe the train was headed by an un-rebuilt Bulleid Pacific, possibly No. 34051 *Sir Winston Churchill*, which earlier that year I had watched cross the bridge over Lambeth Road as it eased away from Waterloo at the head of its sponsor's funeral train. Having patiently congregated and quietly kept our counsel, suddenly those in uniform came to attention and we fell silent. The engine eased the train to a halt and within a couple of minutes a door opened, the Queen and Prince Philip stepped down and, having shaken hands with the Prime Minster, they progressed in front of us towards their waiting car.

Images of members of the Mumford and Rowe families appeared in several newspaper reports the following day and my mother obtained prints of two of the press photographs as a record of this rather odd and, given the security requirements that accompany any public event these days, relaxed occasion.

It was not just the Royal Family Len brushed shoulders with, when the opportunity arose, he was also keen to rub shoulders with railway royalty. It was Len, presumably over a half of bitter at Brunswick House, who learnt *Mallard* was to be transferred to the short lived Museum of Transport at Clapham. He told me the record-breaking engine was going to arrive by rail in Nine Elms Goods Depot, close to the LSWR's original London passenger terminus, and then be transferred by road to the museum. So, late one evening in February 1964, I assume it must have been a Friday or Saturday, with no school the following morning, I found myself standing next to Len in Nine Elms Lane waiting for the action to start.

We were part of a small crowd that had gathered and could see arc lights in the yard beyond the gates to the goods depot. I recall we had a considerable wait but eventually the iron gates were swung open and a small contingent of police officers halted the nocturnal traffic. I can remember there was a bus in the small queue that quickly developed, as very slowly a Pickfords articulated lorry hauling a low-loader trailer upon which *Mallard* had been secured came into view. There was a separate truck and trailer behind on which her tender was poised. Very slowly the lorry began to edge out of the yard and began a wide right hand sweep, so it could head up Nine Elms Lane and into Wandsworth Road. The sleek black nose of the famous engine was now clearly visible and as the trailer turned, her flank and cab clad in LNER blue livery came into view and then there was a lurch, followed by shouts of alarm and then silence. The lorry and trailer had come to a halt and it was immediately apparent *Mallard* had developed a significant list to starboard.

For several minutes it was not apparent what had happened, but like many others we walked around to the opposite side of the vehicles and saw the front offside wheels of the trailer had caused the road surface to subside and *Mallard* was at risk of being pitched on to her side. Quite quickly the number of people present increased with men who had been inside the yard appearing and additional police officers arriving. Nine Elms Lane was now blocked and the increasing number of vehicles that had been paused were firmly stuck. Len quickly expressed the view that someone needed to get on to Nine Elms Shed and procure a set of hydraulic jacks, because he could not see how else the load could be stabilised, let alone moved. He expressed that view to several of the assembly including a police officer, but Len had been retired for several years and his opinions no longer carried weight or influence.

We stayed a short while and I enjoyed close up views of *Mallard*, but it was late in the evening and, wary of missing the last bus, we departed the scene. I remember being surprised there was little mention of the event in the media, although I believe the South London Press carried a story. I never found out how they solved the problem, but I suspect Len's solution was eventually considered if not actually pursued.

As well as members of the Royal Family, boat trains from Southampton regularly delivered the great and the good to the capital city and I have a photograph of Len assisting the actress Valerie Hobson, the wife of the soon to be disgraced politician John Profumo, as she disembarked. For a while this picture became a party game, because we could not at first identify the celebrity Len was receiving.

Inevitably, given his pedigree, Len's time at Waterloo drew to a close. He was in his mid-fifties and promotion to the office of station master was clearly attainable. His own notes indicate

**Len greets the actress Valerie Hobson as she arrives at Waterloo.**

he was promoted to Station Master of Holborn Viaduct, Blackfriars and Elephant and Castle stations on 1 October 1947, on a 'Compensatory' basis. Over the years I heard a number of family rumours regarding Len's final promotion. He told me he had hoped he might be posted to Brighton and indicated he had held on in the hope that position would become vacant, turning down other possible placements. Quite recently a cousin told me his parents had reported Len had been offered Bournemouth Central, but my grandmother had refused to move to that resort. Certainly Holborn Viaduct, while not as busy or aesthetically attractive as the two seaside locations, was convenient. There was no need to move home and Len and Lily stayed in their flat in Walworth. Instead of taking the Tube, Len would now walk to Elephant & Castle Station and catch a train from one of his stations to his office in the small terminus tucked between ancient and modern office buildings in the City of London. He actually reported for duty at Holborn on 28 February 1949.

Two of the stations under his control no longer exist. In Len's time Holborn Viaduct and Blackfriars had two key reasons for their existence; allowing commuters who worked in the City of London access to and from their place of work, and the distribution of newspapers, which were then still produced and printed in and around Fleet Street, a matter of yards from each station.

I was born in 1951 and have very clear and precise recollections of visiting Len at Holborn Viaduct and on several occasions catching with him the 5.02pm Sevenoaks service, which he regularly caught on his homeward journey. My mother used to take me to the long defunct Gamages Department Store in High Holborn, partly because of the vast model railway it contained, and we would then walk up Holborn Viaduct to the station. Len would leave us in his office and the telephone would then ring with him enquiring of me what time the next train to Elephant & Castle would depart. I, of course, would reply 'five-two'.

This was something of an event, because neither my parents nor grandparents had a telephone in their home. Indeed, I recall spending an evening with my grandparents when there was a knock on the door. It was one of Len's staff who had come to tell the 'Guv'nor' there had been a derailment in the goods sidings at Herne Hill and the line to Loughborough Junction was blocked. Len slipped on his full length steam and rain proof coat and set off to catch a bus to the scene of the incident. He did not return that evening. The same scenario would have played out when he was called to the scene of the tragic Lewisham rail disaster in December 1957, which severely damaged the bridge taking the Catford Loop line over the main South-Eastern main line and I understand he did not come home for thirty-six hours.

As I grew older, I sometimes accompanied Len to work and had the thrill of riding in the cab of a 4-SUB unit from the Elephant into Holborn Viaduct. The goods station on the south side of Blackfriars Bridge was then still in use and there was a frequent stream of freight trains crossing the long since dismantled western Blackfriars railway bridge over the Thames. Some of them served the Midland Railway coal sidings in Amelia Street, Walworth, no more than two hundred yards from our block of flats and we could hear the exhaust of the tank engines and the clanging of the wagons as they deposited their cargo down the chutes into the bunkers below.

On one visit to Holborn Viaduct, Len led us down a staircase located toward the end of platform 1 – in those days there were still five platforms in situ – which brought us out on to the up platform of the long defunct Snow Hill Station. To a small boy, standing in the half light at the point where the narrow platform passed from daylight to darkness was challenging. The twin tracks curved down into the smoky darkness and every few minutes there would come the throaty beat of a tank engine battling up the gradient, emerging briefly into the light shrouded in the dense clouds of steam that had accumulated in the tunnel. As the engine rumbled past and headed up the bank

A rare shot of Len at Holborn Viaduct Station. It would appear 'C' Class No 31102 was heading a rail tour as the only steam workings out of Holborn during Len's stewardship would have been newspaper services. *(No record of this engine on a tour has been found on the 'Six Bells' website.)*

towards the ruins of Ludgate Station, the caravan of wagons rattled by, ringing our ears before the beat of the exhaust of the banking loco tagging on behind drowned out the clamour of the trucks. The banker, black, dank and rusty, would wheeze by us before, as it approached Holborn signal box, its ascent completed, giving a blast on its whistle as it eased off the back of the brake van. It seemed only a moment before the banker had eased over the cross-over and was heading back into the gloom to regain its position in the siding by the widened lines at Farringdon to await the next southbound freight.

Northbound freights were not nearly as exciting. No banker was required and the engine would ease into view as it approached the signal box, which straddled the tracks leading to the tunnel. The approach was akin to a child gingerly approaching a steep slope and not wanting to lose control and start running. The engine would slip by down into the tunnel, steam escaping from various orifices with the wagons dutifully following, their wheels grinding and squealing as the curve took effect before, finally, the red lamp on the rear of the brake van would disappear from view.

I needed a change of clothes and a thorough wash when we returned home that day. If only I had been old enough to own and use a camera. Through rose-tinted glasses, I appreciate now what a railway adventure that was, but I know I found the noise and fumes quite frightening as I gripped Len's hand and stood beside him on the narrow, greasy platform.

After he retired, Len took to regularly spending Sunday mornings in Blackfriars Signal Box. It was located on the south side of the river, close to the old goods station. Several times I accompanied him. We would take a bus from Walworth Road to Blackfriars Road and then ascend the carriage road that was originally built to provide street access to the goods station. Len would assume his familiar pose, leaning on the console containing the levers and I would perch on a stool watching what traffic there was on the Sabbath, mainly passenger, slip past. I was always fascinated by watching the progress of those services on the track diagram above the lever frame. Len would sip coffee and chat with his former colleagues and sometimes, before we started home, we would amble through the disused goods station, in which I recall one or two decaying vans were stored. In those days the dome of St Pauls still stood proud and erect at the pinnacle of the City's skyline and we would peer across the two railway bridges at the original Blackfriars Station, drab, sooty and dilapidated, while to its left and a few hundred yards distant, the carcass of the former Ludgate Station could be glimpsed.

Travelling on the railways with Len during his retirement could be entertaining. He always gave short shrift to what he perceived as poor practice by his successors. Len would always travel by train when he could. So, while he could have caught a number 2 bus from the end of the road which would have taken him directly to Vauxhall and Brunswick House, Len's regular visits to the 'Club' were always facilitated by taking a train from Herne Hill or West Dulwich to Victoria, then another train to Clapham Junction, from where he could take a further train to Vauxhall. His concessionary pass meant all these trips were free, but I am certain his main reason for rejecting the bus was his desire to travel on the railway whenever he could.

After my family moved to West Dulwich in 1966, day trips to Hastings meant catching a local service from West Dulwich to Orpington, then a connecting service to Sevenoaks where we could pick up the Charing Cross to Hastings bone-shaking diesel electric service. I did once suggest it might be easier to go up to London and catch the Hastings train at its port of origin, but I think for Len, making all the connections was part of the pleasure of the journey. It is a joy I have shared down the years.

His plans were knocked out of kilter one evening at St Leonards Warrior Square station, where we arrived after our day by the sea to find all services out of Hastings were subject to delay and possible cancellation. We stood on the crowded platform for a considerable time, during which a couple of trains emerged from the tunnel – there are tunnels at both ends of this station's platforms – and both times the young porter, who was manfully loading the destination boards into their holder and making announcements, got it completely wrong. So, people who had pushed toward the platform edge expecting a stopping service to Brighton via Eastbourne, would hastily be alerted by a panicked corrective announcement

**Sunday morning, Blackfriars Signal Box.**

when the headcode on the cab of the incoming train emerged from the tunnel confirming it was in fact a stopping service to Tonbridge. After this had happened twice Len's patience expired and he approached the harassed young man, flashing his concessionary pass as if he were a detective inspector showing his warrant card and firmly enquired whether the telephone in the sentry box the attendant was occupying was working. The startled young man hesitantly replied it was and Len politely suggested he called Hastings Station periodically to ascertain the order in which trains would be departing westward. As this conversation progressed silence descended amongst those nearby and I did felt a shade embarrassed, but the phone receiver was lifted and the two following services, the latter being the London train we had been awaiting, were correctly announced.

**Royalty at Waterloo.**

The delay on the Sussex coast meant our planned connections could not be made and our journey home became protracted. Eventually we found ourselves on an Orpington to Victoria service and a weary calm had overtaken us all. It was dark and the train shuttled from station to station. Upon arrival at one station, a few doors slammed open and then shut and belatedly an announcement was heard confirming the destination and calling points. 'That's Fred', Len pronounced and quickly reminded his wife precisely who Fred was. The train began to move and Len got to his feet, hauled down the window and leant out. 'Alright, Fred?' he shouted as our compartment passed the startled railway man. 'You all right, Guv'nor?' came the strangled reply as the lights of the station faded into darkness. 'Good man', Len commented as he retook his seat and I reflected how Len had startled two Southern Region employees that evening.

I began my legal career in November 1971, twelve years after Len retired. I worked for twenty-nine years in Holborn and became one of the thousands of commuters who crossed the concourse at Holborn Viaduct. By then there were only three platforms in use and finally that was reduced to two. Throughout the day there were the core half-hourly services to Wimbledon and to Sevenoaks (via the Catford Loop), but in the rush hour additional destinations, such as Orpington, Dartford and Gillingham, were added. But there was a definite atmosphere of decline. I would report details of my journeys to and from work and what I observed on the way to Len. By then my parents and grandparents were living in West Dulwich and the starting point for my train journeys into London was either Herne Hill or West Dulwich.

Several times Len told me of meetings he had attended during his stewardship of Holborn Viaduct and its environs, where he had raised the possibility of passenger services resuming through the Snow Hill link from Farringdon to Blackfriars. He told me when he first worked at Waterloo before the First World War it was possible to catch a train in Hampstead or Highbury and travel through the heart of the City to Clapham Junction, Wimbledon and Richmond without changing. He gave the impression his views had fallen on deaf ears. By the time I started my commuting the freight line through Snow Hill tunnel had fallen into disuse with the tracks lifted and the second railway bridge over the Thames at Blackfriars demolished.

I often wondered what Len's reaction would have been when, less than ten years after his death, it was announced that just such a new rail link was to be created and the Thameslink service was established. That development did mean the closure and demolition of Holborn Viaduct, a process which I as a constant observer, found fascinating, and the creation of the new City Thameslink Station. Somehow, as I remembered those increasingly distant excursions to his old hunting grounds and our conversations about his long career, I suspected there would have been an element of 'I told them so' in his response.

*(Unless stated otherwise, all the images accompanying this article are from the collection of Michael Rowe.)*

# Mr Drummond's LSWR 4-4-0s

## Jeremy Clarke

Drummond 'S11' No 395 photographed when brand new at Nine Elms in 1903. Cross firebox tubes were fitted – see the rectangular protrusion on the firebox immediately beneath the spectacle plate. Originally intended for duties on the Portsmouth and West of England lines, their sphere of activities widened post-grouping to include the Central Section of the SR and also duties west of Exeter. All ten engines were superheated from 1920 onwards, at first with the Eastleigh variant and later with the Maunsell type from 1929 on. Smokebox wing plates were later removed. All ten of the type passed to BR but were early casualties, nine going in 1951 and the last, No 30400, soldiering on until October 1954. It steamed to its own demise at Ashford in the same month and was consigned to history in February 1955. *Barry Curl collection*

Dugald Drummond left his post with the Caledonian Railway in 1890 and set sail to take up an appointment in Australia. A consortium had been put together in response to a requirement for locomotives for the New South Wales Government which proposed to order a minimum of seventy-five engines *per annum* for five years. But the project was unsuccessful and in 1891 Drummond returned to Scotland, founding D. Drummond & Son which, in 1901, was incorporated as the Glasgow Railway Engineering Company by his sons, who had been in charge following Drummond's departure in 1895. Orders for locomotives were thin, though in time the business tended to concentrate successfully on making parts such as springs, wheels, axles and axleboxes. (It seems it may have had connections with the engineers William Beardmore. The company ceased trading in 1959.) Hamilton Ellis comments that ordering an engine from Drummond must have taken some nerve, especially setting the specification. Conducting business in the company's Westminster offices, the Drummond *fils* were, presumably, less intimidating.

Drummond had no truck with compounding but the apparent freedom of running in an uncoupled engine as propounded by Francis Webb aroused his curiosity. William Adams had endowed the South Western with four groups of very fine express engines which gave Drummond the opportunity to delve into experimental engineering and test Webb's theory. Webb had, of course, used three or four cylinders but with compounding. Drummond went for four cylinders too, but with simple expansion. However, he seemed to have lost all sense of proportion when it came to the ratio of boiler heating surface to cylinder swept volume. Though ostensibly more powerful than anything that had previously run on the LSWR they could not compete with the Adams 'High Flyers' in terms of either economy or sustained output. Nevertheless, Drummond did not consider introducing another express class, the 'T9', until 1899. In the interim the class 'C8' came into service between June and November 1898.

It is tempting to label the 'T9' as the best of the 4-4-0s but before doing so it should be recalled there were more of the class than any other having the same wheel arrangement and in addition the others, whilst perhaps not having so much of the limelight, also worked for several decades. This view, again from Barry Curl, depicts No 305 complete with original wing-plates, cross tubes, no superheater and seemingly made ready for a special working. It later received SR livery as E305 in February 1924, the 'E' suffix being dropped nine years later in 1933. It was later an early casualty when withdrawn in April 1951.

This was intended for semi-fast work, its cylinders and boiler being as in the earlier 'M7' and '700' classes. The 'C8' was clearly based on Drummond's '476' class, built particularly to work the joint Midland/NBR 'through' services introduced in 1876 over the North British Railway's Carlisle-Edinburgh 'Waverley' route. Four of that class came at first from Neilson, eventually twelve in all, for its time a large and powerful engine, a necessity, given not just the long and steep climbs to the summits at Whitrope and Falahill but the line's constant curvature. Times had changed however and the weight of rolling stock with them. Even on the work for which it was designed, the 'C8' suffered from insufficient boiler power because of the relatively small firebox. There were only ten members of the class, numbered 290-9.

As to dimensions, the cylinders were 18½"x26" and driving wheels 6'7" in diameter on a 9'0" wheelbase. The boiler, pitched at 7'9" above the rails and pressed at 175psi, contained 1,068sq ft of heating surface with the firebox, which had a grate area of 20¼sq ft, adding a further 124sq ft. The engine, weighing in at 46t 16cwt, had a tractive effort of 16,755lbs at the usual 85%BP. At first the class was allied to six-wheel 3,500 gallon tenders weighing 40t 16cwt when full, but were later provided with 4,000 gallon 'water-carts' which turned the scales at 3 cwt short of 45 tons. The class was rather overshadowed by the mixed-traffic 'K10' and 'L11' engines that followed it at the beginning of the 20th century, seemingly being passed around the sheds with a regularity that suggested nobody wanted them. Perhaps as an indication of their limited usefulness, withdrawal began with No 294 in February 1933 and concluded with 298 in January 1938.

The class that followed the 'C8' could arguably be termed Drummond's *'pièce de resistance'*. Dubs & Co produced the first 'T9' in February 1899, and followed it with twenty-nine more to January 1900. They were numbered 702-19/21-32. (The 'missing' no, 720, was allocated to the sole class 'E7' 4-2-2-0 of August 1897.) Nine Elms built 'T9s' at the same time though the first did not appear until June. In typical fashion numbering tended to be haphazard, if generally in batches. The Works turned out Nos 113-122 between June and September 1899, Nos 280-9 from October to February 1900, Nos 300-7/10-4 between January and May 1901, and Nos 336-8 in the September and October following, by which time sixty-five of the class were in service.

There were differences between batches. The thirty Dubs engines had firebox water tubes and tenders as attached to the 'C8'. The twenty built at Nine Elms in 1899-1900 had those same six-wheel tenders but were without the firebox water tubes, though those appeared in the final Nine Elms fifteen of 1900-1. That batch uniquely had full width cabs and splashers and eight-wheel 4,000 gallon water-cart tenders weighing 44t 17cwt. They also had steam sanding with the boxes in the smokebox delivering the sand between the bogie wheels. All, however, were later converted to gravity-sanding in line with the other class members. Steam reversers were common throughout.

Driving wheels and cylinders in all cases were as in the 'C8', but the main difference between the two was to be found in the boiler. The coupled wheelbase being extended to 10' permitted the firebox also to be lengthened to provide a grate area of 24sq ft. Heating surface was thus increased to 1,335sq ft to which the firebox water tubes, where fitted, added another 165sq ft. With a pressure of 175psi the tractive effort also matched the 'C8'. But the enlarged boiler granted the 'T9' a performance the earlier class could not sustain. Weight varied slightly depending on the presence of the firebox water tubes but in general the engine came in at 48t 17cwt.

Dubs must have been much impressed because the company sought and obtained permission to build another example, completed in December 1901, for exhibition at Glasgow and Newcastle. It came to the South Western with its superb exhibition finish and the number 773, though renumbered 733 in 1925 to make way for a new Maunsell 'Scotch Arthur', *Sir Lavaine*.

By the end of 1907 all engines were hauling water-carts though ten of the later Nine Elms batch were given six-wheel tenders in 1925 on transfer to the Southern's Eastern Division. Six more of the class were similarly modified in 1928 for Central Section work; water-carts were banned from these parts. The absentees had returned to the Western Section by 1940 though not all of the sixteen recovered their water-carts: no 726, for example, was still running with a six-wheeler in 1949.

Thirteen engines were converted to burn oil under the Government's 1947 scheme. They were Nos 113-5/8/21,280/6, 303/5/14 and 713/22/31, also fitted with electric lighting at the same time. Popular and efficient though they were, the scheme was dropped in 1948. With conversion in full swing it occurred to the Treasury that paying the price for oil in dollars when the country was already deeply in dollar debt to the USA, and the pound had been severely devalued against that currency, made continuing with the scheme unsustainable. None of these engines worked again though their official withdrawal did not begin until March 1951, Nos 280 and 714 being the first out. It would appear Nos 121 and 286 actually received their BR numbers.

Superheaters were fitted to all members of the class between June 1922 and July 1929, the Eastleigh version up to 1924, the Maunsell type thereafter though that was later substituted for the former version. As with all Drummond engines given superheaters by Urie and Maunsell, the smokebox was extended and mounted on a saddle. The cylinder bore was increased to 19" at the same time but other changes were more obvious, a stovepipe chimney seated on an extended smokebox for example and the loss of firebox water tubes from boilers so fitted. In this condition the heating surface was reduced to 1,063sq ft, the Maunsell superheater adding another 213sq ft. Weight went up to 51t 16cwt and the tractive effort to 17,678lbs at 85%BP. It is perhaps too much to claim superheating galvanised performance but it certainly made an already good engine into a very good one. The pseudonym 'Greyhound' had already been applied, for the additional power over the Adams 'High Flyers' gave the 'T9' the ability to get away with a real smartness. Moreover, for all that the 'Flyers' were much liked by their crews, the 'T9's inside cylinders diminished the hunting to which their predecessors were sometimes prone.

'T9' No 336. Post-grouping the class might be seen throughout the system, basically anywhere from Dover to Padstow and all places in between. Those working away from the original turf were generally also fitted with 6-wheel tenders. ( Is that an LBSCR tender attached to No 336?) *A. G. Ellis*

O. S. Nock has published logs of a number of runs with the class, two of them providing a contrast between the work of superheated and non-superheated engines between Waterloo and Southampton. The schedule for the 79.2 miles was 92 minutes. No 313, in original condition, had a gross load of 390 tons which would appear to be close to the limit for the engine on this timing. The maximum noted speed to Woking, where the engine was already 2½ minutes late, was 57mph at Weybridge, and this had fallen away to 42½mph at MP31. It had recovered only to 57mph on the level through Farnborough and had again fallen away below fifty on the slight rise through Winchfield to Hook. Basingstoke was thus passed 4½ minutes down though speed had recovered again to 55mph. As this was on the uphill stretch towards Worting Junction it would appear some sort of check may have been experienced prior to Hook though no note of this was shown. Though a half-minute has been recouped by Worting, and despite 71mph being registered at Shawford, the train was more than six minutes late at Eastleigh. But there must have been an element of 'recovery time' in the schedule as Southampton West was reached exactly four minutes late.

**No 30721 of the same class recorded at Eastleigh on 23 March 1957 attached to Bulleid 3-set No 721 and a motley collection of other vehicles. The headcode would indicate a Salisbury to Portsmouth, via Eastleigh, working. No 30721 had a life of just less than fifty-nine years when it was withdrawn in July 1958, by which time the influx of more modern 'Standard' designs had seen a number of the older 4-4-0s withdrawn.** *Tony Molyneaux*

**Light engine movement for No 30300 on the up line between Shawford and Shawford Junction. The 6-wheel tender carries a goodly amount of coal and will no doubt have also been well 'watered'. 28 March 1957.** *Tony Molyneaux*

By comparison, superheated No 336, with 380 tons gross, was master of the work. Surbiton was passed at 60mph though the train was through Woking a half-minute late: MP31 was cleared at 48mph. All but a minute had been gained to Basingstoke and that was retained at Worting Junction where speed had fallen only to 44½mph. Nothing higher than 70mph was needed at Shawford to ensure an arrival at Southampton a little more than 1½ minutes early.

Under BR the 'T9' was power-classified '2P' at first but '3P' later. In their heyday the engines were allocated to main line depots such as Nine Elms, Bournemouth, Dorchester, Salisbury, Exmouth Junction and Eastleigh. As time passed they became more widespread with Yeovil, Basingstoke, Fratton, Plymouth Friary and Guildford housing them as well as the already notified sojourns on the Southern's Eastern and Central Section. The greater number finished their working days nominally at Exmouth Junction though generally outposted to the various sheds on the Southern's 'Withered Arm'. Perhaps the regard for the class is best shown by use for years of two of its members as the South Western's and, indeed, the Southern's, 'Royal' engine. No 119 was the first, the only one to retain malachite livery throughout the war. On its withdrawal in December 1952 the mantle fell on No 718, and though kept clean that engine never received a comparable finish although maintenance was top class.

The transfer in numbers to Eastleigh from the end of the 1950s was a herald to mass withdrawals, completed, almost, with that of No 287 from there in September 1961. Yet not quite, for by that time No 120 had been selected for preservation in the National Collection. The dated withdrawal of this engine, also from Eastleigh, is shown as July 1963.

The South Western was never required to carry the massive volumes of heavy freight that its counterparts north of the Thames had to handle. But there never seemed to be enough engines that could turn their hands to moderately-loaded trains be they passenger or freight. Adams's 'A12' class, the 'Jubilee', was the first proper design in that category but Drummond continued with the 4-4-0 theme when he came to consider the requirement.

The first seven of the forty-strong class 'K10', Nos 153, 329/40-4, left Nine Elms in December 1901. The next year saw the remaining thirty-three in traffic, numbers being 345/7/80-94 and 135-46/9-52. These engines closely resembled Drummond's celebrated class '80', the 'Coast Bogies', introduced on the Caledonian Railway in 1888. But the cylinders were the common LSWR size ones at 18½"x26", and the boiler, firebox and grate area were as in the 'C8', though the firebox water tubes brought the heating surface up to 1,291sq ft. The 5'7" driving wheels were on a 9'0" wheelbase. At 85% of the boiler pressure of 175psi the tractive effort was 19,756lbs. The engine

The fate of the 'T9's in later years was undoubtedly to take on some duties to which they were hardly suitable. Apart from local passenger services on various cross country routes, they might also be found on pick-up freight working, hardly ideal for an engine fitted with a steam reverser. Ever so, this is what an unidentified member of the class was so engaged in at Nursling on 2 April 1957. *Tony Molyneaux*

No 383, a member of the 'K10' class. The location is not given but from the multitude of rails we can safely assume around the area of Clapham Junction. The headcode gives three possible alternative services all from/to Waterloo Windsor (via loop line), Hounslow and Feltham including trains terminating at Barnes, or Southampton via Alton. No 383 had a life of forty-seven years and ceased to be used in 1951.

In basically original condition but now with a degree of workaday grime, the photograph is not dated but in consequence of the condition, might it be reasonable to assume post-1914? No 136 would never receive a BR number, indeed only one of the class ever did, No 30382, whereas the engine depicted was one of nine laid aside in 1947, although thirty-one did pass to British Railways, with the last going in 1951.

weighed 46t 14cwt in working order. When new, thirty of the class had second-hand six-wheeled tenders weighing 40t 16cwt. These had been relinquished by 'C8' and 'T9' engines which instead took the new 4,000-gallon water-carts originally intended for them. The remaining ten 'K10's had new six-wheelers of the same design. The class acquired the nickname 'Grasshoppers' but this was modified on the appearance of the other 'mixed-traffic' class, the larger if very similar 'L11'. That also attracted the name but the two were differentiated by size into 'Small Hoppers' and 'Large Hoppers'.

Here is No 382, seen in Southern days at Yeovil. Another member of the class, No 340, reposes behind 'G6' No 238. Wing plates and cross tubes removed, clamps added to lower half of smokebox door.

91

The 'L11' was to the 'K10' as the 'T9' was to the 'C8'. Nine Elms turned them out rather less swiftly than it had the 'K10', the engines appearing in batches over a period of four years from May 1903. Numbers were spread through the stocklist as usual, being 134/48/54-75/405-14 and 435-442, forty in all. Cylinders and driving wheels were the same as the 'K10' but the coupled wheelbase was extended to 10'0" as in the 'T9' to provide for the longer firebox, and the boiler contained 1,500sq ft of heating surface to which the firebox water tubes contributed 165sq ft. Engine weight in working order was one hundredweight over 51 tons.

New water-carts were built for them but only Nos 174/5 and 407-13 benefited, the remaining new tenders being filched by 'C8' and 'T9' engines which gave up their six-wheeled ones in exchange. Further tender exchanges post-Grouping saw all but two of the 'L11s' equipped with water-carts while six-wheelers were more common behind the 'K10s'. The excepted 'L11s' were Nos 440/1 which also had dual-braking until the mid-1930s. None of the eighty 'Hoppers' was ever superheated though several acquired Urie stove-pipe chimneys complete with capuchon. Both classes could be found all over the South Western though the 'K10' was the more common of the two west of Exeter.

Wartime saw several 'K10's lent to the LMS. Five went in 1941 to work around Bristol and Gloucester, receiving any necessary repairs at Derby. Three more moved to Nottingham in 1944 but had returned south by the end of the year. Three of the Bristol five were also back on home turf by 1944, the other two returning in 1945.

Fifteen 'L11s' were scheduled for conversion under the oil-burning scheme but only eight, Nos 148/54/5/7/70/2/411 and 437, were so equipped, having electric lighting installed at the same time. As with the others taking part in the scheme they never worked again following its conclusion.

Only 'K10' No 382 received its BR number as did just eighteen of the 'L11s'. The first noted withdrawal was of 'K10' Nos 136/49 and 342/4, all in January 1947, though the 'L11s' were complete until Nos 439 and 440 went in May 1949. Both classes were extinct by August 1951 when 'K10' No 384 was withdrawn from Yeovil shed. The last 'L11' had succumbed two months previously, No 409 of Exmouth Junction. Would they have lasted this long but for the outbreak of war? Who knows, though they were certainly outclassed by the time it ended and probably much worn out too.

The 'Hoppers' had proved ideal for semi-fast passenger services over the Salisbury-Exeter switchback and with that in mind Drummond designed a larger version, the ten members of class 'S11' being introduced between June and December 1903. Numbers were 395-404. This was, in effect, an 'L11' with 6'0" driving wheels, a slightly larger boiler of 1,550sq ft. including firebox water tubes, pitched 8'6" above the rails, and cylinders bored out to 19" diameter. At 85% of the usual 175psi pressure, tractive effort came to 19,391lbs. The engines weighed 52 tons and were paired with 4,000 gallon water-carts weighing 44t 17cwt. These contained feedwater heaters of 382sq ft though the engines were apparently still provided with injectors. It may be noted too that these were the first locos to be fitted with Drummond's patented balanced crank axle.

'L11' No 408 at Nine Elms soon after entering service. Forty were built at an average cost of £2,000. In reality they were a stretched 'K10' slightly longer and with a 'T9' boiler. The engine is coupled to a 4,000 gallon tender. Intended as an improved 'K10' whose performances were not all that might have been expected, they worked well on semi-fast and relief duties.

SR days with No 409 now minus wing plates and cross-tubes. Several of the class were attached to six-wheel tenders when new but these had all been substituted for the eight-wheel version by 1926. The class was extinct when the last three were taken out of service in June 1952.

Power-classed '2P' under BR, much of their early work was, as designed, west of Salisbury. Nock has published a run with No 398 timed by R. E. Charlewood in 1908. The train was the 3.30pm from Waterloo, scheduled to leave Salisbury at 5.9pm on a 96-minute run to Exeter. The load was only 210 tons but without checks of any nature the train was 1¾ minutes late into Queen Street. The 17½-miles to the summit at Semley were completed in 22½ minutes from the Salisbury start at a respectable 46mph. But the very favourable four miles down to Gillingham that followed did not see the speed rise beyond 68mph. Compare that with runs by two 'T9's where speeds of 77½ and 78½mph had been achieved. Much the same applied at Sherborne which the 'T9s' passed at 78½ and 80½ while No 398 managed just 70mph. (Did the smaller wheels really make that much difference? After all, the front ends of the classes were very similar.)

There is unfortunately neither timing nor speed noted at mp113½, though the engine made a reasonably fast, but not outstanding, climb up through Templecombe. Similarly the engine climbed well through Crewkerne to Hewish summit, mp133¼ being cleared at 30mph. Note that the two 'T9s'

'S11' 4-4-0 No 404 modified by Urie. A superheater is now fitted, although, as with other engines so modified, the trade off meant less room on the front framing, which made the disposal/cleaning of the smokebox at the end of a run all the more difficult. *A. G. Ellis*

mentioned earlier, and both hauling 240 tons, passed at 32½ and 34½mph respectively. Charlewood makes no note of the speed at Axminster, near the finish of the 13 miles down through the Axe valley. But the station was passed in 64¾ minutes from the start and though no scheduled intermediate timings were shown it would seem that No 398 was close to 'right time'. It is also annoying that no time was taken at Honiton summit, (mp153½), cleared at 22½mph, but intermediate timings of other engines over the climb would indicate No 398 found it hard. For example, by mp152½ it had lost more than 1½ minutes in the 4¾ miles from Seaton Junction to one of the 'T9s' hauling 30 tons more. Both the 'T9s' were into Queen Street ahead of time and are credited with a net figure of 94½ minutes.

Robert Urie fitted his superheaters to all of the class from 1915, removing the firebox water tubes at the same time. Boiler heating surface was reduced to 1,154sq ft, the superheater adding 195sq ft. Maunsell installed his own version with 213sq ft of surface as renewal became necessary. Weight went up to 53¾ tons.

The class went as a whole to the LMS between 1941 and 1945, working mainly on the Somerset & Dorset though it is recorded that they did get rather further afield than that most picturesque of railways. Post-war the engines returned to very secondary duties with Basingstoke, Fratton and Guildford being among the sheds housing them. From the latter they worked over the splendidly scenic Redhill-Guildford route below the North Downs. Nos 395 and 401 were the only members not to be renumbered by BR with No 402 the first withdrawal, in February 1951. However, the last, No 400, did not leave Guildford shed until October 1954, outlasting all its brethren by a month short of three years. Incidentally, in their later days the engines were fitted with short stovepipe chimneys, some with a small capuchon, to make them available for work off the Western Section.

The next development was the fairly obvious one of providing the 'S11' with 6'7" driving wheels. This, the 'L12', the 'Bulldog', was a big step forward from the 'T9', the engines becoming real favourites with their crews. Twenty numbered Nos 415-34 were turned out by Nine Elms between June 1904 and March 1905. The advance was less on the basic measure at the drawbar and more on the additional power in the boiler. The main structure was just as in the 'S11' but the 6'7" driving wheels brought the tractive effort back to 17,673lbs. The same 4,000-gallon water-carts with heaters were provided though this class had use of pumps rather than injectors.

In the same way as with the 'S11s', the 'L12s' had been fitted with Urie superheaters by 1922 and all were later superseded by Maunsell's variety with 213sq ft of heating surface: that of the boiler was reduced to 1,154sq ft. Nos 415/23/4 were made oil burners in 1921 for a time and the process was repeated with 415 and 424 together with No 426 in 1926, reconversion followed.

No 421 was the engine involved in the derailment of an Up Plymouth Boat Train at Salisbury in June 1906. The curve through the station, and particularly the 10-chain reverse curve through pointwork at the east end, had a generous speed limit of 30mph imposed throughout. The engine had, as usual, taken

**A Drummond 4-4-0 at work away from its original haunts. This is 'L12' No 422 at Bromley on 20 August 1938.** *H. C. Casserley*

Of all the 4-4-0s, the ten comprising the 'D15' class had the greatest visual symmetry with the bigger Drummond 4-6-0 types. The reason for this has to be the high pitch of the boiler. In consequence it might be thought they could well have had a tendency to roll at speed but this does not appear to be mentioned by Bradley. In common with other Drummond designs, shared similarity includes the cab, firebox, splashers and smokebox. *Barry Curl collection*

over the train at Templecombe. Following complaints of 'risks' being taken and evidence of running ahead of time, Drummond had made it plain that further continuance would be severely dealt with. Driver Robins, a very experienced man, was well aware of this, as was made plain by his comments to staff at Templecombe while he awaited his train. But after a poor start in which four minutes were lost in the twenty miles to Dinton, signal box records show Robins covered the next 8½ miles to the point of derailment at an average of 72mph. At Salisbury no attempt appeared to have been made to conform to the speed limit, meaning the engine was thrown out of gauge on the reverse curve at the east end and crashed into a milk train passing on the down line. Twenty-four passengers on the train – half its complement – Robins and his fireman, Gadd, as well as the guard of the milk train and the fireman of a light engine standing on the down bay platform line, were killed, twenty-eight in all, the most in any accident on the LSWR. As a comment on the solidity of Drummond engines in general No 421, despite turning over at speed in the crash, was so little damaged it was taken on its own wheels to Nine Elms for repairs.

What went through Robins's mind is impossible to know of course. However, it transpired this was the first time he had run through Salisbury without stopping and the first time he had worked this train. Anecdotal evidence suggests he must have been aware from conversations with other drivers that timekeeping demanded some hard running. Moreover, passage of Salisbury is followed by ten miles of climbing to mp73¼ at Grateley, so it is not too much to suppose he aimed to get some momentum for that. Oddly, this was one of three similar night-time accidents occurring in a little over a year, the others being at Grantham and Shrewsbury. As the engine crews perished in those too the reasons for them also remain a mystery.

To happier things: a run from Salisbury on the 3.30pm ex-Waterloo with 'L12' No 431 in 1907 was also apparently recorded by Charlewood. The load was again of 210 tons though the timing was 98 minutes rather than the 96 of the others. This was to take account of the maximum permitted speed through the restricted layout at Yeovil Junction; this was eliminated by reconstruction in 1908.

The engine topped Semley at 45mph and had accelerated to 75 at the bottom of the dip at Gillingham, the subsequent climb through Templecombe to mp113¼ bringing the speed back to 45mph again. The train was through Sherborne at 76mph and after observing the Yeovil slack topped Hewish at 32mph. Rather like the 'S11', speed at Axminster was only 69mph whereas all three 'T9s' shown in the lists went through at 80mph or slightly more. Nevertheless the engine climbed well to Honiton summit, topping it at 28mph. Unfortunately a PWS at the exit to the tunnel made for a slower recovery but with a speed of 80mph at Broad Clyst, the highest on the journey, the train was into Queen Street only fifteen seconds late, accorded a net of 97¼ minutes.

Ten of the class went to the Eastern Section in the 1930s for which shorter stovepipe chimneys and reduced height safety valves had to be fitted. Tender swaps were also necessary, six wheelers being surrendered by the 'Hoppers' in exchange for the water-carts. Some of these engines later went to the Central Section but all were back on home ground immediately prior to nationalisation. By that time they had long been superseded on the best work. The first withdrawal was of No 430 from Guildford shed in March 1951 and, incidentally, the only one of the class not to show its BR number. That same year, apart from No 429 at Basingstoke, the class was sheltered at only three sheds, Fratton, Guildford and Eastleigh. All were withdrawn that year other than Nos 415 and 434. The former held out at Fratton until January 1953 while No 434 managed to escape the axe until February 1955. One can only surmise that working out of Guildford shed – which had a reputation for keeping its engines in very good order – along that delightful line to Redhill, kept it young at heart.

*In BR days the class remained active around the Eastleigh area and were frequently employed not just on local workings but also, as seen here, with No 30472 at Fareham on a through service from the Western Region in June 1951, just seven months before it was taken out of service. Dennis Callender*

Having been diverted by his doubtful excursions into six-coupled express engines, Drummond returned to the 4-4-0 for what turned out to be his swansong and a fitting finale to his work, the 'D15' class. The Uries, Works Manager Robert and Chief Draughtsman David, hoped to persuade Drummond to make some innovations including piston valves, Walschaerts gear (the one being concomitant with the other) and superheating. Only the last did not get the nod, the usual smokebox steam dryer being installed instead. (This probably raised the temperature by no more than 20°C.) The boiler, pitched 8'9" above the rails, was the same as in the new one provided to the double-single No 720 in 1905, though the firebox had a sloping grate of 27sq ft area rather than the flat one of that engine and the 4-6-0s. There was 1,704sq ft of heating surface to which the firebox water tubes contributed 170sq ft: pressure was raised to 200psi.

The cylinders had the usual 26" stroke but with a diameter of 19½", the steam being supplied through piston valves of 10" diameter. Driving wheels were the standard South Western ones of 6'7" and, at 85%BP, the tractive effort was 21,275lbs. The coupled wheelbase remained at 10'0", but at 24'9" the overall wheelbase was 18" longer than that of the 'L12' and the 'T9'. Weight in working order went up to 59¾ tons. Water-cart tenders were supplied but these were second-hand 4,500-gallon ones which had turned out to be inadequate for the thirst of the 'T14' 4-6-0s introduced in 1911. (These had new ones holding 5,800 gallons and weighing no less than 60 tons 8cwt.) The feedwater heaters in the ex-'T14' tenders had 382sq ft of surface which required the engines to be fitted with pumps.

The ten engines in the class, numbered 463-472, came into service from the new locomotive works at Eastleigh between May and December 1912. Unfortunately Mr Drummond did not live to see them all, dying at his Surbiton home on 8 November that year. Like many other South Western men he is buried at Brookwood cemetery. The engines were an immediate success, working the heaviest expresses on the principal main lines to Bournemouth and Salisbury. As with others, Urie added superheaters but quite early on, all being so fitted by 1917, the firebox water tubes and steam driers naturally being removed at the same time. The heating surface was reduced to 1,285sq ft to which the superheater added 231sq ft. (In Southern days the Maunsell superheater of 252sq ft superseded it.) But the boiler pressure was reduced too, to 180psi, bringing the tractive effort down to 19,147lbs. The cylinders were later bored out to 20" diameter, raising the tractive effort again to 20,142lbs.

A number of runs on the Bournemouth line have been published including a most remarkable effort made in the early 1920s. This was by No 470 on a 2¼-hour up express timed by the Rev L. A. Garrard. In this case we know the name of the

*Sister engine No 30471 arriving at Fareham from the direction of Cosham with a Portsmouth to Salisbury working, via Southampton. No 30471 remained at work until February 1954, after which just three remained 'on the books' with the last, No 30465, going in January 1956. Dennis Callender*

driver, Bullard of Bournemouth shed. The load was no less than 416 tons tare and an estimated 440 tons gross. A time of 37 minutes was allowed to the only intermediate stop, at Southampton West [Central]. The engine got to 60mph at the bottom of the dip towards Christchurch but not unnaturally fell away on the sharp climb through Hinton Admiral to pass through at 41mph, still a remarkable effort with the load. Some brisk running through the New Forest continued with a top speed of 65½mph at Brockenhurst which saw No 470 come to rest at Southampton in an actual time of 35m 20secs.

What followed next was just as impressive though a slow recovery from the Northam slack meant the engine had dropped 42 seconds on the ten minute timing to Eastleigh, passed at 48mph. A grand climb followed, an average of 41.6mph being achieved over the 17.3 uphill miles from Eastleigh to Litchfield box, passed at 39½mph. Clearly not winded from the climb, the engine recovered well, taking only nine minutes to clear Basingstoke (8½ miles), and making an average of 62.3mph over the forty-three miles from Litchfield to Wimbledon and a maximum of 72½ at Hook. Signal delays in the final stages meant the train was 4¾ minutes late into the terminus though the net was estimated at 95 minutes. Considering the load there can be nothing but admiration for the work of driver Bullard and his fireman. (Incidentally No 470 was another engine subject to oil firing in 1921 and 1926.)

More typical perhaps of the loadings generally handled was one of 325 tons gross brought up from Southampton by No 468. The train was on time at Eastleigh though a relatively leisurely climb to Litchfield box, cleared at 41½mph, saw 1¼ minutes lost to Basingstoke. But from there the engine averaged 65½mph to Wimbledon, a maximum of 72 being recorded at Byfleet, though signals in the final stages caused a late arrival of 1½ minutes on the 92 minute schedule. The Rev. Garrard estimated the net as 91½ minutes though I think this is a little harsh and would certainly knock at least a half-minute off that.

New 'King Arthurs' 4-6-0s displaced the 'D15s' from the Bournemouth line in 1925/6 and instead they went to Fratton for work over the Portsmouth Direct. They lost their water-carts then, being given 3,500-gallon six-wheelers instead. Though timings were relatively moderate on the route, the class later shared the best work with the 'Schools' until both were displaced by electrification in 1937. Their final express work, on which they were very popular with the Nine Elms crews manning them, was mainly the Lymington boat train service, though No 463 did not see this. It was the only one of the class to be converted to oil burning in 1947 and as with all the others so equipped never worked again when the scheme was terminated. Officially withdrawn in December 1951 it never received its BR number.

Towards the end the class was concentrated principally at Eastleigh though No 471 was at Fratton and Nos 467 and 464 at Nine Elms. The latter had a final fling on the RCTS 25th Anniversary Special on 28 June 1953. The driver was the redoubtable Bert Hooker, himself an RCTS member. The load of 245 tons was taken down the Windsor lines to start with but once crossed to the Main and on the move Hooker found

97

*A reminder of times past. 'C8' No 292 possibly on a Bournemouth line service running via East Putney. Barry Curl collection*

the steam reverser would not hold its position. Nevertheless he managed, he stated, to keep the engine running sweetly. Other than that, little was said about the journey, though a speed of 78mph was noted at both Andover and Porton. Bert commented rather wistfully that, but for the reverser playing up, the run in general could have been better and the line speed limit of 85mph possibly reached. The first of the engines to go other than No 463 was No 469, also in December 1951, No 465 being the very last, in January 1956.

How to sum up? As a body the 4-4-0s gave good value for money except perhaps for the 'C8', which turned out to be 'nobody's baby'. Certainly the 'L12', the 'D15' and, most of all, the 'T9', proved to be in the forefront of express loco development in their time, the 'T9' in particular, especially with the benefit of superheating. And yet Nock, for example, draws a comparison between the 'T9' and Maunsell's rebuilds of the Wainwright 'D' and 'E' classes and finds the 'T9' wanting. That was, of course, in his book outlining the history of the SECR. But having lived on all three Sections/Divisions of the SR/BR(SR) I'm afraid I'm with Ossie, which makes me think it ironic that a 'T9' is in the National Collection but one of that really exceptional class, the 'E1', is not.

## Bibliography

'Drummond Locomotives, A Pictorial History', Brian Haresnape and Peter Rowledge, Ian Allan Ltd, 1982.

'The London & South Western Railway', O. S. Nock, Ian Allan Ltd, 1965.

'The South Western Railway', C. Hamilton Ellis, George Allen & Unwin, 1956.

'The Drummond 4-4-0s and Double Singles of the LSWR', Locomotives Illustrated No 44, 1985.

'Locomotives I Have Known', J. N. Maskelyne, Percival Marshall, 1959.

'A Further Selection of Locomotives I Have Known', J. N. Maskelyne, Percival Marshall, 1962.

'Twenty Locomotive Men', C. Hamilton Ellis, Ian Allan Ltd, 1958.

'History of the Southern Railway', C. F. Dendy Marshall, Rev R. W. Kidner, Ian Allan Ltd, 1963.

'Richard Maunsell, An Engineering Biography', J. E. Chacksfield, The Oakwood Press, 1998.

'Bert Hooker, Legendary Railwayman', A. E. 'Bert' Hooker, Oxford Publishing Company, 1994.

'Red for Danger', L. T. C. Rolt, Pan Books, 1966.

'The South Eastern & Chatham Railway', O. S. Nock, Ian Allan Ltd, 1961.

'An Historical Survey of Southern Sheds', Chris Hawkins and George Reeve, Oxford Publishing Co, 1979.

'Railway Track Diagrams No 5', Southern & TfL, TRACKmaps, 3rd ed. 2008.

'Gradients of the British Main Line Railways', Ian Allan Publishing, 2016.

'ABC of Southern Locomotives', Ian Allan Ltd, various editions 1942 onward.

Net sources include Grace's Guide and SEMG websites as well as others where confirmation of data from other sources may need to be confirmed. I should add that there are occasional differences noted between sources of, for example, cylinder size, heating surface and tractive effort. Steering a path has thus been a little difficult at times but I have taken the majority view and recalculated TE where there has clearly been an error in the mathematics.

# Back to the Future

Fifty-two years ago the electrification of the Bournemouth line services out of Waterloo signalled the end of steam on the Southern Region. The full story of this monumental event is told in detail in the latest 'Southern Way Special Issue: No 16 – 50 Years of the Bournemouth Electrics' compiled by commuter and enthusiast Colin Scott-Morton.

As a taster as to its content we are delighted to present a small selection of additional images recently come to light through out friends at Transport Treasury – *but you will still have to read Colin's new book for the full story!*

One of the precepts of the modernisation of the route was the compatibility of the new EMU and Push-Pull stock with the locomotives used on the line, illustrated here with a new TC unit on its way from York to Eastleigh behind (Class 33) D6518 and temporarily held at signals outside Basingstoke. The old era in the form of locomotive hauled stock is seen in Barton Mill carriage sidings alongside.
*Alec Swain/Transport Treasury.*

99

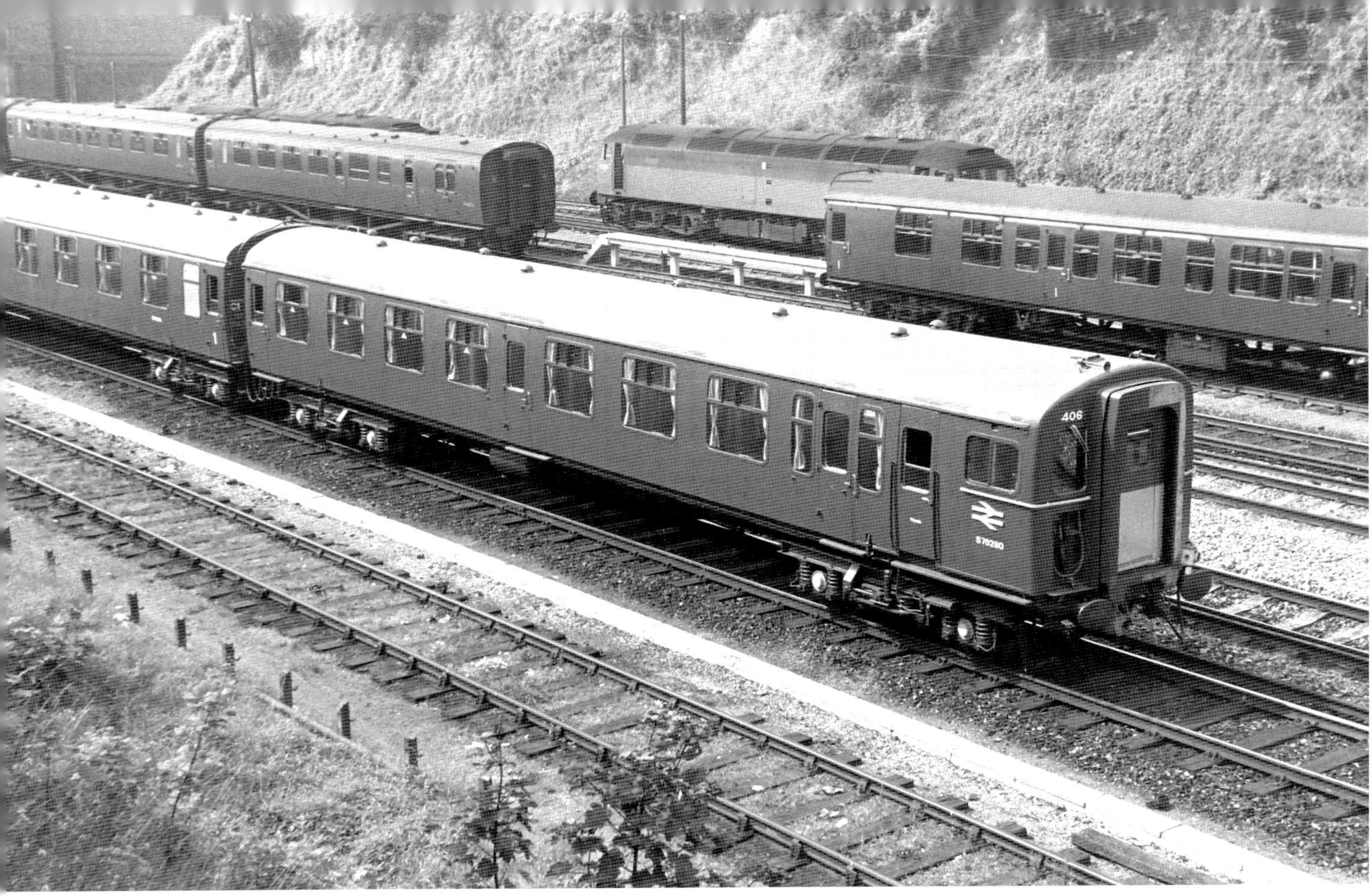
406
S76280

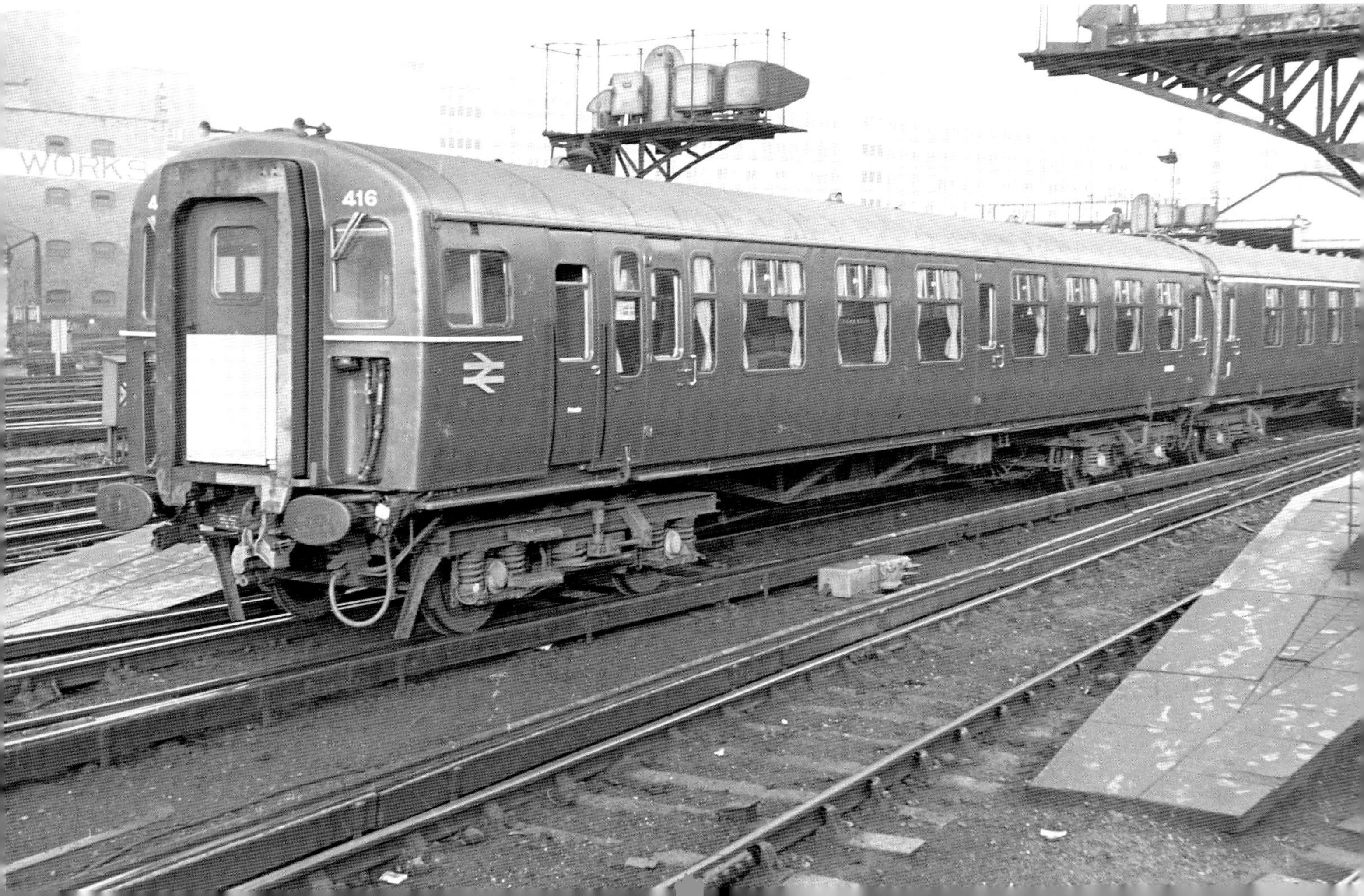
WORKS
416

*Above:* **'ED' (Electro-Diesel) No E6016 at Clapham Junction.** Designed with flat sides so as to comply with the restricted loading gauge on some of the South Eastern lines, the class were one of the undoubted successes of the third-rail electrification era and paved the way for duel voltage and duel power units in the future. Although seen here on freight, this type of traffic would quickly fall away and the class would spend most of their Southern Region life on passenger and parcels workings. *Alec Swain/Transport Treasury.*

*Right:* **Class 33 and Class 71 conjoined and able to be controlled by a single man.** *Alec Swain/Transport Treasury.*

*Opposite top:* **The rear end of the same TC unit; No 406, but note the steam era oil lamp at the rear as well. For those with a shorter memory the coaches were painted in all-over 'Rail-Blue' relieved with cast aluminium 'double arrows' and orange curtains.** *Alec Swain /Transport Treasury.*

*Bottom:* **Test run at Waterloo and now with the double-red blank in use instead of the oil lamp.** *Alec Swain/Transport Treasury.*

The Southern Way                                                                                                              Issue 48

The ultimate Push-Pull, a Class 33 (at the time still in the D65xx series) at Bournemouth with units either side, again the class could be controlled by a driver at one end of the 'TC' set. No date, but likely to be have been a test/shunt move and certainly prior to the full electrification service as conductor rails have yet to be laid. *Alec Swain/Transport Treasury.*

For stopping services the 4Vep units were introduced. 'Five-a-side' seating in what was then deemed Second Class was not universally popular but there could be no doubt these sets would whisk the passenger from start to stop at speeds undreamt of behind steam. Belying its ability at sprinting, No 7712 waits at Fleet with an up service. (The '43' headcode may not be strictly accurate as this refers to 'Portsmouth to Southampton via Netley' which route was at the time non-electrified and so still operated by diesel traction.) *Douglas Twibell/Transport Treasury.*

# Southern Way Special Issue No.16
## 50 YEARS OF THE BOURNEMOUTH ELECTRICS 1967-2017

### Colin Scott-Morton

Much has been written about the end of steam, but what came after it has received rather less attention. Whilst the electrification scheme which ousted steam was carried out 'on the cheap', it was ground-breaking in many ways, not least in representing the first example of high speed push-pull operation of passenger trains in the UK. And in one sense, it was also the end of another era, for while third-rail electrification continued to be used on various Southern 'infill' projects in later years, and much more recently, on TfL's London Overground network, the Bournemouth scheme represented its last installation on a long-distance main line.

This book looks back at the original implementation of the scheme, and at all that has happened during the five decades since.

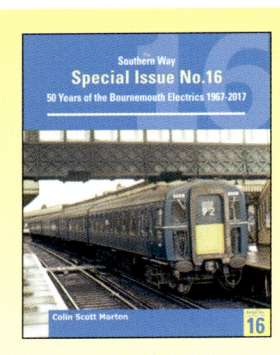

**ISBN:** 9781909328914
**Binding:** paperback
**Dimensions:** 273mm x 215mm
**Pages:** 144
**Photos/Illus:** over 175 photos and maps
**Price:** £16.95
**Publication Date:** November 2019

# Book Review
## *LBSCR Carriages, Vol 3', Bogie Stock 1879 – 1907*

**Written by Ian White and published by the HMRS**

Southern (and constituent) aficionados will no doubt already be familiar with the two earlier volumes in this series both published by Kestrel Railway Books.

Now the mantle has been taken over by the Historical Model Railway Society and it is pleasing to note that whilst the cover may be to a different style the page size is identical, meaning that they sit well together on the bookshelf.

As the title says, this is Vol 3 – a further volume is scheduled for later. Within the present book 230 pages, nine chapters (including a supplement to the first two volumes), eight appendices, references, diagram numbers and an alphabetical index describe the vehicles of the company between the dates stated, supplemented by 143 black and white illustrations, tables, and 122 plans mostly to 4mm scale. The whole is produced on good quality art paper. With a paucity of early carriage views generally – most photographers of the period concentrated on the 'locomotive three-quarter' view – the author is to be congratulated on his spread of images. Despite also the often common feature of utilising previously-seen imagery from other works, Mr White is to be praised in locating numerous photographs not previously seen including works detail and, where necessary, contemporary restoration views which depict features that would otherwise go unseen.

One very minor comment, and this is of course subjective, is that I thought the cover design was not perhaps to the standard of the earlier volumes. I would hope this would not put off any potential purchaser for within there really is a 'box of delights'. Highly recommended.

ISBN 078-1-64516-144-8 £29.95. (HMRS members £19.95.)

*The next instalment of 'Salisbury – Exeter' has been held over for no reason other than lack of space. We intend to include this as soon as possible.*

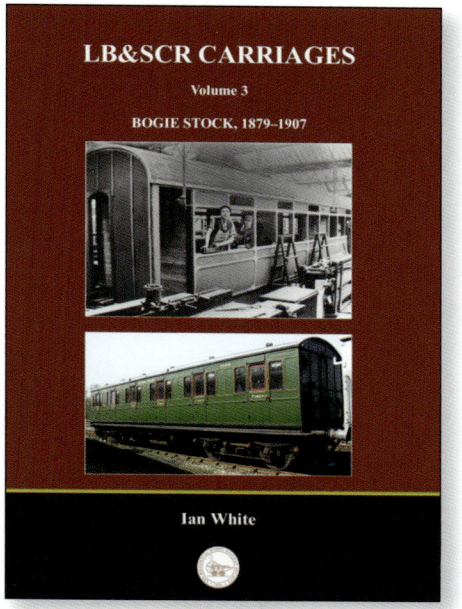

# The Southern Way

The regular volume for the Southern devotee

## MOST RECENT BACK ISSUES

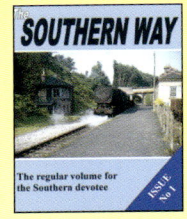

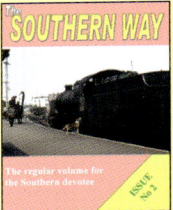

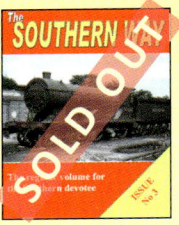

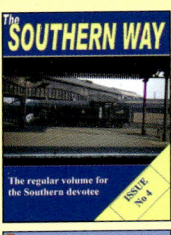

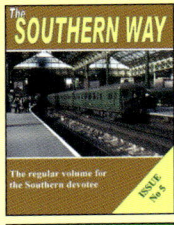

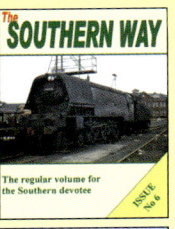

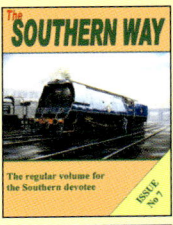

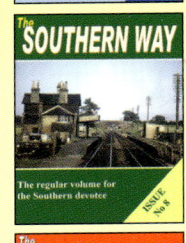

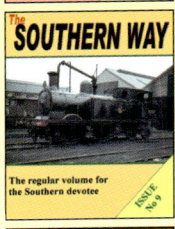

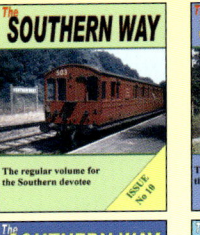

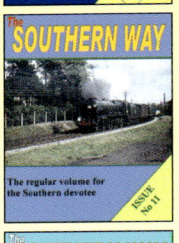

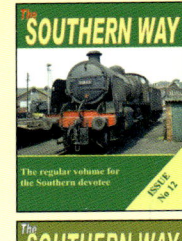

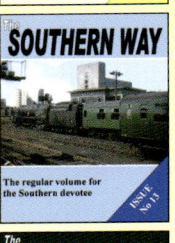

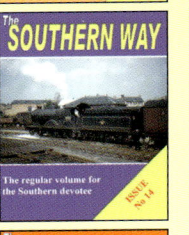

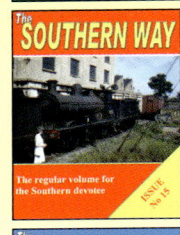

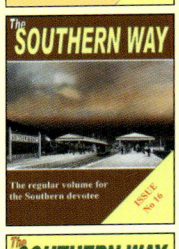

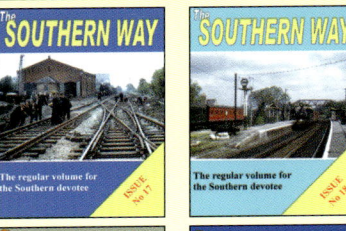

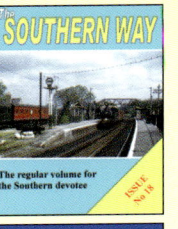

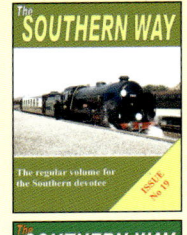

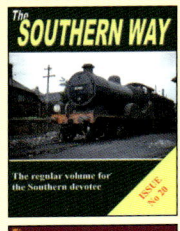

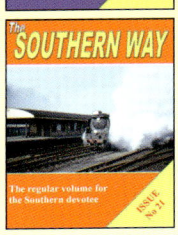

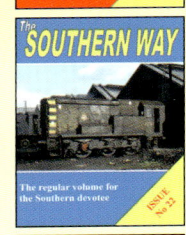

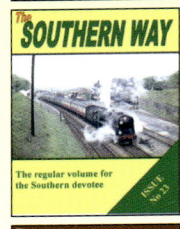

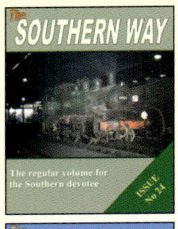

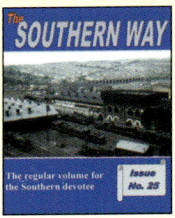

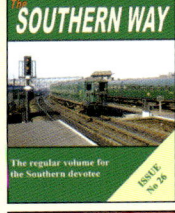

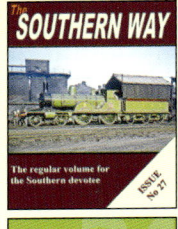

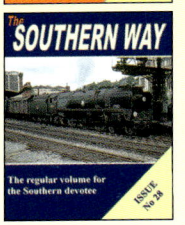

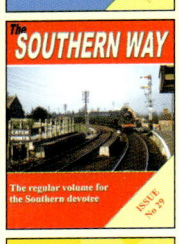

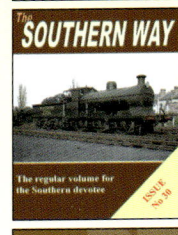

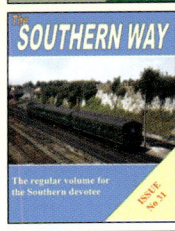

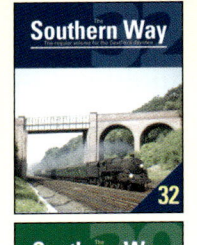

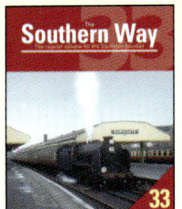

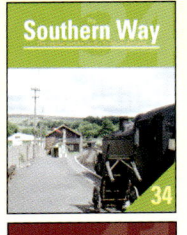

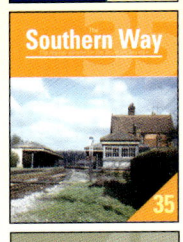

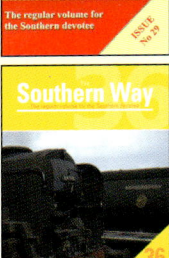

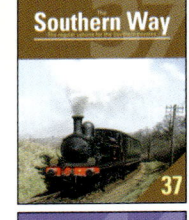

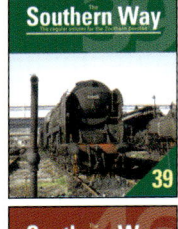

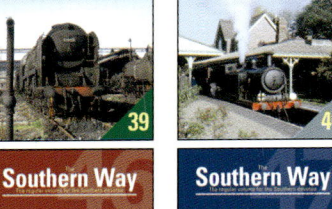

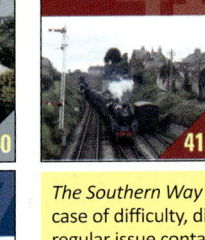

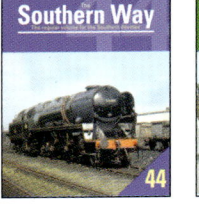

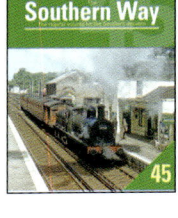

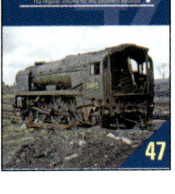

*The Southern Way* is available from all good book sellers, or in case of difficulty, direct from the publisher. (Post free UK) Each regular issue contains at least 96 pages including colour content.

£11.95 each
£12.95 from Issue 7
£14.50 from Issue 21
£14.95 from Issue 35

Subscription for four-issues available
(Post free in the UK)
www.crecy.co.uk